DON'T SAY
I DIDN'T
WARN YOU

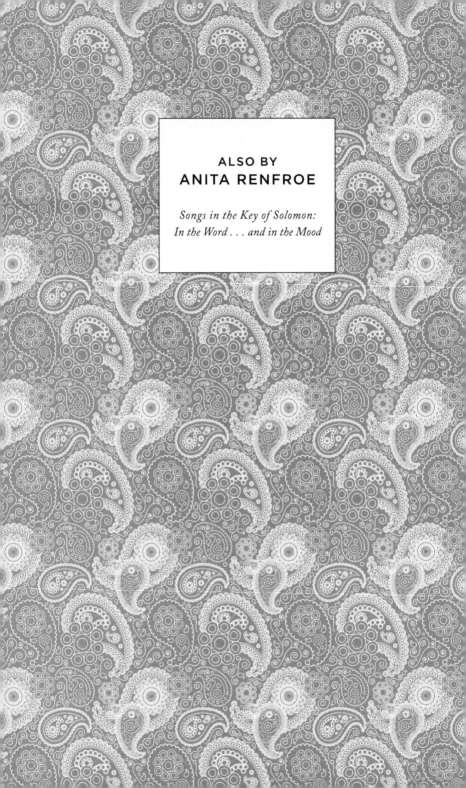

ALSO BY
ANITA RENFROE

Songs in the Key of Solomon:
In the Word . . . and in the Mood

DON'T SAY I DIDN'T WARN YOU

Kids, Carbs, and the Coming
Hormonal Apocalypse

voice

HYPERION
New York

Library of Congress Cataloging-in-Publication Data

Renfroe, Anita
   Don't say I didn't warn you : kids, carbs, and the coming
hormonal apocalypse / Anita Renfroe.
      p. cm.
   ISBN 978-1-4013-4098-8
   1. Christian women—Religious life.   2. Motherhood—
Humor.   3. Mothers—Religious life.   I. Title.
   BV4527.R448 2009
   248.8'43—dc22

                                             2009012671

Hyperion books are available for special promotions and premiums.
For details contact the HarperCollins Special Markets Department
in the New York office at 212-207-7528, fax 212-207-7222, or email
spsales@harpercollins.com.

Design by Karen Minster

FIRST EDITION

10   9   8   7   6   5   4   3   2   1

THIS LABEL APPLIES TO TEXT STOCK

For my family,

without whom I would not know love

(or have material)

CONTENTS

ACKNOWLEDGMENTS

This is normally the section of a book reserved for meaningful personal words of gratitude or shameless, flagrant sucking up. I can multitask.

Buckets of love and gratitude go to my family. My husband, John, discussed at length in multiple chapters because our lives have been intertwined for twenty-seven anything-but-boring years, is the very best thing that ever happened to me—although I believe he does not like to be referred to as a "thing."

My children, Calvin, Austin, and Elyse, have been the love of our lives since they were just zygotes and are all beautiful, talented, and inspiring to me every day. I am also proud to say that our first-round draft pick for Team Renfroe, Lisa, is a beautiful addition to our family and I look forward to lots of new material from being a mother-in-law.

I would also love to thank my mother, who has believed that I was special from my first breath. My dad and grandmother, who have passed from this life, were constant cheerleaders, and their spirits still infuse my everyday living with words that continue to reverberate in my heart. Thank you, JC and Vesta, for embracing me in your family.

Special thanks to Kim for enduring friendship—and to Jean, Ginny, Stacy, Nancy, Kay, Ellie (and all the Pink Sneaks), all the WoF Porch dwellers, Patsy, and

Jan: Women need women friends and I am blessed to have you in my life. For Mrs. Maizey James: Thank you for praying for me without ceasing. As I have said before, I depend upon it.

A big, big dollop of thanks to the Voice team, especially to Ellen Archer for believing that this book might be a good idea and to Barbara Jones for her guidance in shaping a bunch of random writings into something that made a lick of sense.

Mike Atkins, Tony Johnsen, and Joanna Burgess: Thank you for taking care of business so that I don't have to worry my pretty little head about it. And Alan Clarke—you are the master of the fine print and much beloved because of it!

Love and more love to my church, Destiny Metropolitan Worship Church, and to Dr. Bryan E. and Lanette Crute. It is a joy to serve together.

Finally, all thanks to God from whom all blessings flow.

DON'T SAY I DIDN'T WARN YOU

The "Mom Song"

**Sing to the "William Tell Overture,"
music by Gioachino Rossini**

Get up now

Get up now

Get up out of bed

Wash your face

Brush your teeth

Comb your sleepy head

Here's your clothes

And your shoes

Hear the words I said

Get up now

Get up and make your bed

Are you hot?

Are you cold?

Are you wearing that?

*Where's your books and your lunch and your
homework at?*

Grab your coat and your gloves and your scarf and hat

Don't forget you've got to feed the cat

Eat your breakfast

The experts tell us it's the most important meal of all

Take your vitamins so you will grow up one day to be
    big and tall

Please remember the orthodontist will be seeing you
    at three today

Don't forget your piano lesson is this afternoon

So you must play

Don't shovel

Chew slowly

But hurry

The bus is here

Be careful

Come back here

Did you wash behind your ears?

Play outside

Don't play rough

Would you just play fair?

Be polite

Make a friend

Don't forget to share

Work it out

Wait your turn

Never take a dare

Get along

Don't make me come down there

Clean your room

Fold your clothes

Put your stuff away

Make your bed

Do it now

Do we have all day?

Were you born in a barn?

Would you like some hay?

Can you even hear a word I say?

Answer the phone

Get off the phone

Don't sit so close

Turn it down

No texting at the table

No more computer time tonight

Your iPod's my iPod if you don't listen up

*Where you going and with whom and what time
    do you think you're coming home?*

Saying thank you, please, excuse me

Makes you welcome everywhere you roam

You'll appreciate my wisdom

Someday when you're older and you're grown

Can't wait 'til you have a couple little children
of your own

You'll thank me for the counsel I gave you so willingly

But right now

I'd thank you NOT to roll your eyes at me

Close your mouth when you chew

We'd appreciate

Take a bite

Maybe two

Of the stuff you hate

Use your fork

Do not burp

Or I'll set you straight

Eat the food I put upon your plate

Get an A, get the door

Don't get smart with me

Get a grip

Get in here, or I'll count to three

Get a job

Get a life

Get a PhD

Get a dose of . . .

I don't care who started it

You're grounded until you're thirty-six

Get your story straight

And tell the truth for once for heaven's sake

And if all your friends jumped off a cliff

Would you jump, too?

If I've said it once, I've said at least a thousand times
*   before that*

You're too old to act this way

It must be your father's DNA

Look at me when I am talking

Stand up straighter when you walk

A place for everything

And everything must be in place

Stop crying or I'll give you something real to cry about

Oh!

Brush your teeth

Wash your face

Get your PJs on

Get in bed

Get a hug

Say a prayer with Mom

Don't forget

I love you

KISS

And tomorrow we will do this all again
     because a mom's work never ends

You don't need the reason why

Because

Because

Because

Because

I said so

I said so

I said so

I said so

I'm the Mom

The mom

The mom

The mom

The mom

Ta-da

Words by Anita Renfroe Copyright © 2007 Bluebonnet Hills Music/BMI

INTRODUCTION:

YouTube, iTube, We All Tubed, Apparently

The phone was ringing, it was still dark outside, and you know that adage about how "a phone call between midnight and sunup can't be good news"?

I was appropriately jangled.

"Somebody from *Good Morning America* wants to talk to you," my husband, John, said.

I heard his words and understood them, but they made no sense. It was one of those moments when a woman is absolutely sure that her husband must be fitted for a hearing device, and soon.

I squinted to try and make out the numbers on the digital clock. This was before my LASIK surgery so I couldn't tell if the first number was a five or a six, but it was early; there was a little drool on my cheek.

"Hi, Anita. So sorry to call so early but I'm a segment producer for *Good Morning America*. One of our newswriters got the YouTube clip of your "Mom Song" routine from a friend and showed it to Diane Sawyer. Diane loves it, so we were wondering if we could have your permission to play a portion of it for our watercooler segment this morning."

Immediately, I was awake. Fully awake. Red Bull awake. "Uh, sure."

"Could you send us a printed copy of the lyrics so that Diane and Robin can read them while the clip is playing?"

"Uh, sure."

"We will be using it around seven-thirty if you want to watch."

If I want to watch? IF I WANT TO WATCH? The morning had now moved from Best Possible Dream Sequence to Alternate Universe.

I grabbed my robe and hurried downstairs to e-mail the lyrics to the producer and tried to run through the people on my "Must Call if *Good Morning America* Ever Calls You Super Early in the Morning" list, and quickly realized that only my mom, my manager, and the Beach Girls (my set of friends who get together at the beach every year) would be happier than angry if I called before 7 A.M. So after phone calls to the handful-of-people-I-can-awaken-at–any-hour-without-retribution, my husband and I sat up in bed, drinking coffee and laughing about how a phone call between midnight and 6 A.M. might, occasionally, be good news, after all.

And this all started because of a case of comic envy.

You see, about a year before *Good Morning America* called, I heard a comic friend of mine, Justin Fennell, perform a song in which he revisits an exhaustive list of places he has eaten, sung to the Johnny Cash tune "I've Been Everywhere." It was something that no one else in his right mind would even attempt because the list of places Justin had eaten was so long and tricky to remember, much less spit out, and I thought *I wish I had something like that!*

I hate to admit that the piece that put me on the general national consciousness radar was hatched from a bad case of envy, but it's true. I mean, I'd envied other things: a great handbag, the ability to wear four-inch heels to a party and survive more than ninety minutes, someone's totally ripped abs, a friend's nonexistent pores, an all-inclusive vacation, but this was a brand of envy I had heretofore not known.

I've been doing what I call "estrogen-flavored stand-up musical comedy" for a dozen years now. I got my start not in comedy clubs but by doing funny songs for women's groups at church-sponsored events. I can't begin to tell you the number of things I have eaten that were crustless, contained poppy seeds, or were served on three-tiered trays. Among church ladies the food and themed decorations are the star attractions; the day's speaker is sometimes an afterthought.

Still, these church-sponsored women's events provided a good setting for me, since: (a) I am a woman and most of the comedy I purvey is for women, and (b) I love an audience full of women. There are simply far more things about women that are similar than are different, and my brand of comedy celebrates those things. My comedy is also clean, just because that's who I am and I want my comedy to reflect who I truly am, not some persona I adopt for stage purposes. If you come to see my show, it's really just a version of what you would get if we sat down to talk over a cup of coffee. Okay, maybe the musical numbers are extra; they might be pretty weird in a Starbucks.

Anyway, in the months before I saw Justin's Johnny Cash routine, I had been wanting to do a stand-up bit about how repetitive and reflexive the things are that mothers say day after day after day after stinkin' day. I had compiled (with the help of some friends) a list of the stuff I knew I said and the stuff they said and the stuff our mothers had said to us through the years (all of these lists were frighteningly identical). I thought it would be funny if I learned to say all the things mothers always say really fast with only a couple of breaths for the whole piece (the way it might sound to our kids when we're spewing it out, rapid-fire). Wouldn't that be a fun bit for anyone who was a mom—or even if you just *had* a mom? Then I had that moment of professional envy when I saw Justin's song; and the competitive streak in me kept gnawing around the edges of my thinking about the repetitive things moms say.

I tried to think of a tune that embodied the speed at which moms can articulate their mind-numbing rollout of daily advice. The fastest song I knew was "Flight of the Bumblebee," but it's almost impossible to sing to that. Seriously, try it. Unless you know 127 six-syllable words, it can't be done. Well, not at actual tempo. If you slow it down, maybe. So, the next fastest song is Rossini's "William Tell Overture," and as soon as I thought of it, I realized that this music, which kicks off like a trumpet call to the cavalry, pretty accurately reflects how moms attack the day. I found a recorded performance of the piece that worked as a track to sing to, cut out a couple of sections of music, and then rearranged all the mom sayings I had compiled to follow a mom from the beginning of her day until she tucks the kids in at the end.

It took twenty-two years to live that song, two hours to make it rhyme.

When I taped the piece at a live performance a couple of weeks later, it was better received than I had dared to allow myself to imagine. Not only were the people laughing and enjoying the universality of the piece, but they also responded with The Happiest Possible Occurrence in a Performer's Evening: the Midshow Standing O. It's not that rare to get one at the end of an evening (people are appreciative, they're incredibly tired of sitting, *and* they *have* to get up to leave) but to score one in the middle of the concert is rare and exhilarating. The song seemed to hit on a universal truth that almost all moms come hardwired with this loop in their heads.

But an audience of mothers and the daily audience that is my children are not the same. Back at the ranch, my three semigrown kids began to give me grief because, according to them, I was the ONLY comedian ALIVE who did not have a video clip on YouTube.

If I had to post a clip, I thought the "Mom Song" might be a good clip to post. Besides, we were coming up on Mother's Day weekend. Maybe a few hundred people might see it; then we would take it down on the Monday after Mother's Day. So we posted it. About a hundred people saw it. And I was *thrilled*. Until my kids informed me that by YouTube standards the response to my video was *l-a-m-e* and proceeded to tell me (in that tone of voice that implies "you-could-not-be-more-ignorant-if-you-tried") that you have to leave things posted on YouTube for a while so that more people can see it. "Exactly how many more people could possibly see this?" I said. "I don't understand."

But I went ahead and left the video up there, where it languished through a long, hot summer. My kids made it clear that they would think I was even lamer if I weenied out and took down the video. So I left it up. Out of mother-of-teenagers shame.

And, lo and behold, sometime around Labor Day weekend somebody (Maybe it was you. If it was you, thank you.) started forwarding the YouTube link to her friends and suddenly it went from 5,000 hits to 300,000 hits in a matter of days. When I told my kids, they said, "That's *great*, Mom. You're going viral."

Now, up until that moment in my life, when something "went viral," it was not a good thing. "Viral" was any condition accompanied by high fever and stomach cramps; "viral" required fighting back desperately with bottles of Lysol and cases of crackers and Sprite. It was a major head shift for me to embrace the idea of something "viral" being a good thing.

The upshot of my kids' encouragement to post that fateful clip is that they expect way better gifts for Christmas, now that they feel they have made my career happen.

This in no way makes up for the stretch marks.

Thus we arrived at the surreal experience of sitting in bed watching Diane Sawyer and Robin Roberts discuss the video clip one October morning, followed by an inundation of calls from other news and entertainment outlets. Everyone was trying to find out who this mom-ic was and what her story was. Apparently it was a slow news day; Britney and Brangelina must've taken the week off. I had a business manager but no public relations person, so my husband, John, and I were in scramble mode, trying to figure out what to do with the interview and appearance requests that were pouring in. The syndicated newsmagazine show *Inside Edition* offered to pay me to change a ticket to a gig and meet them at the airport; CBS sent someone to camp out on my doorstep to let me know they were serious about their desire to put me on their morning show the following week (like I said, s-l-o-w news week). I flew to New York a few days later and did the rounds (*GMA*, CBS's *The Early Show*, *Fox & Friends*, Gayle King's XM radio show, then on to LA to tape *Dr. Phil*).

I did every one of those shows with no manicure because there wasn't time. *The moral of this story*: Don't skip your nail appointment; you never know when you'll really need it.

In the months that followed, I did comedy spots for *Good Morning America* as their "special comedy correspondent" (a reporter embedded in the front lines of motherhood—protected by Spanx instead of Kevlar) and *The New York Times Magazine* published a feature on me that was amusing because, according to the story, I am an anomaly. The article pretty much said, "OH MY GOSH! SHE'S A CHRISTIAN—AND PEOPLE THINK SHE'S FUNNY! WHAT MIGHT MANKIND DISCOVER NEXT?" Then several networks started talking about a prime-time sitcom (a "mom-com"?) with my life as a premise. So I am currently obsessing about how I will deal with the fact that if a sitcom does happen, HD television will reveal every enlarged pore on my face.

Interviewers sometimes ask how fame has changed my life, which makes me just about spit out my coffee because—really—most people have absolutely no idea who I am. People often know my "Mom Song" but have no idea of the name of the person who made the thing. I have what we refer to as a very high "Oh, her" factor. When people buy tickets to one of my shows and tell a friend, "I'm going to see Anita Renfroe's show tonight," the friend says, "Who?"

"Anita Renfroe, she's a comedian." (Beat. Beat. Blank stare.) "You know, the one with that 'Mom Song.'"

"Oh, *her*!"

Anyway, by way of long book introduction, this is me. I am "*Oh, her.*"

I WOULD ALSO like to take this opportunity to pre-apologize. Not because I am sorry about the things you are going to read in the following pages, but because I have learned this: When it comes to comedy, somebody is going to be offended. That is not my intention; it's just inherent to humor. In order to have something funny to say, you have to have a subject matter to discuss. In the discussion of said subject matter, there will be observations made that are purely subjective and not a statement of facts.

This is the basis of humor.

But lots and lots of people did not get that memo.

So they buy humor books, and then they get mad.

If you are thin, you will be offended when I talk about that. If you are ample, you probably won't get offended when I talk about that because you are more relaxed than your skinny friends who are always hypercaffeinated and revved up because of their fast metabolism. But if you are short, blond, have thyroid problems, don't like chocolate, do have kids, never had kids, do like your mother, don't like her much at all, it doesn't matter, *something* will set you off and you will think, *I can't believe she would write that! I should e-mail her and let her know about my personal experience with _____ and that literally thousands of people suffer with* _____ (fill in the blanks with the ailment, issue, cause of your choice) *and let her know exactly why* _____ *is not funny.*

Since I have no staff of people to read through e-mails, I will just go ahead and offer this pre-apology.

Dear _____

Thank you for writing me about _____.

I hope that the incision from your humorectomy heals up fine and doesn't leave a scar.

Sincerely,

Anita

And, just to cover my bases, here are sundry disclaimers:

- Everything in this book is my own, personal experience.
- Only carbs were ingested while I wrote this, so no foods with actual food values were harmed in the making of this book.
- If you are reading this in a public place where noises are not appreciated (a library, a sleep-study lab, a church service, etc.), I cannot be held responsible for any inappropriate laughter that results.
- And, lastly: If you come and meet me in person at a book signing or a comedy event and I don't look as good as the retouched photo on the cover of this book, you are just gonna have to find a way to deal with that. I cannot pay for the village it took to create that one magical mo-

ment when six people were fritzing with my hair and spackling on makeup, taking light readings and holding various diffusing/softening filters tilted *just so* at my feet, with my face at the perfect angle to minimize my wide nose, my body contorted in unnatural (uncomfortable!) ways to make me appear smaller, and a stylist who found clothes for the shoot that were way better than I normally buy at T.J. Maxx.

Don't say I didn't warn you.

Brother,
Can You Spare an Epidural?

*B*ecause I travel a lot, I get a *lot* of frequent flier miles.

This is not to brag, because—with the state of the airline industry being what it is these days, believe me, these miles mean absolutely next to nothing. Not even a better brand of peanuts. But I do get upgraded on flights that are not on Canada regional jets (which is Canadian for "Tiny Cramped Flying Tube with No First Class"), so I get to sit next to other people with lots of flier miles. It's like our own little club of "I'm Never Home Either" people. They are almost always people who represent companies and are über committed to their work and happy to talk about what they do. This works well when I get them to tell me as much as possible about their life *before* they find out what I do for a living, because once they find out, that pretty much means they are done talking about themselves for fear that something they tell me will end up as material on my next DVD or in a book.

They could not be more right.

There was this guy who sat next to me and told me that he worked in medical technology. This was a nice, general answer, which I found to be of no use to me at all. After I probed a little more, he said that he once worked for a company that made a piece of medical equipment that helped with the birthing process. I was all ears, and what I thought I heard him say was, "It's basically a GPS for the baby while it is in the birth canal."

I cannot begin to tell you how many different directions my brain went at that moment. My head was practically exploding with possible comebacks. *Do babies get lost on their way out that often? How did babies make it out of the birth canal for thousands of years without this technology? How small must that screen be, anyway? Is there that much traffic in there that the baby would have to take alternate routes and avoid tollways? If the satellite was unavailable, would the baby take a wrong turn and come out of an ear? If it's triplets or quadruplets, does that qualify as gridlock?*

I guess the man could see the wheels spinning and the smoke coming out my ears because he interjected something like, "It's a diagnostic tool for the labor and delivery nurses to use so they don't have to perform so many digital checks to see how the cervix is widening during the birth process." I could see how that would be very useful for the L & D nurses who have to pop that glove on fifty times per shift to check the labor's progress.

Apparently, with this technology, some sort of receivers are placed on the mother's abdomen that act as the "satellites" and receive transmissions from the disposable sensors that are attached to two points on the cervix and to the top of the baby's head. So you can actually tell how much the cervix is widening and how far down the baby's head is positioned. If I were an L & D nurse,

I would be writing my congressman for this piece of equipment. Because that digital check thingy has to qualify as one of the worst parts of that job.

For those of you who have never experienced this "check" as a patient, imagine that you are going for your yearly Pap smear and someone has decided to compound the usual procedural discomfort by: (1) allowing you no food or drink for many hours, (2) increasing the circumference of your midsection by 300 percent, and (3) sticking a hot branding iron across your lower back. Now, imagine how you feel as a nurse starts popping a latex glove on her right hand and informing you that she will need to do a "little check to see how you're progressing." This is not only gross, but I would venture to say it is also dangerous for her—like approaching a wild animal in pain. Labor and delivery nurses should receive hazard pay for this part of their job description. I'm sure many have had a foot planted in their face. I know I fantasized about doing it.

I REMEMBER how much I wanted to have a baby when John and I first got married. It was foolish, as we had no insurance and were both still in college at the time. But the combination of youthful optimism and total disregard for the amount of time or money this decision would cost us resulted in a pregnancy that started about the time we had been married five months.

About the only time I ever looked at my middle with admiration was when I was with child. When I found out that I was pregnant, I could not wait to get into maternity clothes. (Little did I know that after child number three, I would never be able to get out of them.) I was pregnant in the 1980s, when we were rocking the navy blue tent dresses with sailor collars and big, red bows, like maybe we were outfitting whales for the navy.

But at least it used to be that when you were pregnant, you had the luxury of wearing tent dresses for a while and not worrying about your body shape for nine months. No more. Due to recent advances in medical science (or celebrity workout routines), modern moms now get pregnant only in the very front. No weight distribution to the butt or hips. Maternity clothes are a good deal cuter now than in the olden days because they are designed to show off your "bump." Notice that the term even implies "little"? When I was pregnant, the mass on the front of me was definitely not a "bump"; it was more like a "planet," with its own "moon" around the backside of the planet.

Modern developments aside, when I first learned that I was pregnant, I was very excited and thought this was going to be the most blessed, beautiful, rose-petals-at-my-feet-and-bluebirds-lighting-upon-my-forearm time of my life.

Until I went for my first prenatal visit.

Which starts with a weigh-in.

These weigh-ins don't seem too bad the first couple of visits because the other person you are carrying inside of you is about the size of a pea. Peas don't weigh that much. In fact, for my first few prenatal visits, I weighed a little less than I ever had, from all the retching. I distinctly recall looking around at the eight- or nine-monthers sitting around the waiting room and thinking, *I'll* never *get that big*.

I could not have been more wrong. By the time I got to my eighth month, my weight had far surpassed the magic number my doctor had recommended I gain, so I would dress in the lightest thing I could find, wear two-ounce flip-flops in the freezing weather, and ask to go to the bathroom twice before I went on the scale. However, there was no denying the number of butter beans and Fudgsicles I was downing. The nurse would slide the metal weight on the balance beam farther to the right, farther to the right, farther to the right until I knew that I had reached the edge of I-Won't-Ever-Get-in-Those-Prepregnancy-Jeans-Again Zone and then loudly pronounced that weight as she wrote it on my permanent record.

Once they've elevated your blood pressure by giving you a number higher than you ever imagined for your weight in your LIFETIME, *then* they take your blood pressure. I don't know how they expect it to be normal when you have just come to the realization that you are really, really *B-I-G*, but if you use your Lamaze breathing techniques (more about that later), you can pant and blow yourself down to a medium-range systolic. This is the real reason why you should pay attention in Lamaze class.

Then they asked me to give a sample. Now, when I am discussing a "sample" at the obstetrics office, I am not talking about a trial-size cosmetic. They want something called a "clean catch." It sounds like a term you would hear in circus training school trapeze class—"Great job, Mr. Wallenda! That was a clean catch!"—but this clean catch entails precise stream-to-cup timing, which is difficult when your reach is hampered by the watermelon in your middle by month number eight. Plus they give you the smallest-size Dixie cup known to mankind, and they expect you to stream into that cup in an efficient manner. There are multiple problems here, one being that, if you did excuse yourself twice in preparation for the weigh-in, you are basically in a Number One deficient status. And there is no more pee being made right now, as all available liquids are being marshaled in support of the other little person you are growing.

The second problem is that the term "clean catch" will never be an accurate description, as you will need to use multiple antiseptic wipes and paper towels in order to accomplish this (not so clean) catch. It's actually quite un-clean. I don't know if other people did this part better than I did, but the clean catch drama every month left me feeling like there must be a better technique than the one I used. And I really would have had a better chance of hitting that cup if they'd given me a thirty-two-ounce Big Gulp cup from the 7-Eleven.

After you have successfully provided a clean catch (which *may* have taken you two hours), you meet your "happy" obstetrical phlebotomist. These are usually women who have lurking latent sadistic tendencies, and they have been given the duty of filling a GINORMOUS vial with blood from your little veins to determine if this pregnancy is going swimmingly or if you need more vitamins. They tie off a little rubber tube at the top of your arm and look for a vein. I always looked away and tried to go to my happy place, but I found that there was no admittance to the happy place when there was a needle sticking in THE TENDEREST PART OF MY ARM.

From these blood tests they determine if you are iron deficient, in which case they give you *even more* iron than is in your normal prenatal horse pill (aka "vitamin"); this way, you can be *even more* constipated. Why do you need this much iron, really?

Do they make you take this much iron in case you happen to be gestating an action hero?

Finally, you make it to an exam room, where you are left with a paper gown and the biggest lie in all of health care: "The doctor will be in to see you in just a minute." After this whopper, you are left to amuse yourself: alone, close to naked, on the vinyl table covered with tissue paper. I found that if I got up and rear-ranged the things on the little cabinet, it distracted me for several minutes and confused the doctor and nurse whenever they finally got around to showing up.

But when you are done with that, you still have fourteen minutes to kill and by your eighth month your back does not want to sit up with no support for more than five of those. So you do what comes naturally; you lie down on that exam table to wait for The Good Doctor. This would be fine if he/she actually showed up "in a minute," but you lie there, and lie there, and lie there, waiting and waiting and waiting. By the time The Good Doctor finally does make it to your room, the combination of the vinyl and the paper and your sweat have created something akin to a papier-mâché that has you good and stuck to that table. And what, pray tell, is the first thing the doctor asks you to do?

"Ms. Renfroe, could you please scoot down toward the end of the table?"

Scoot down? Scoot down! I lay there thinking, *Hey, Sparky—how's about you take that little stool with the little wheels and how's about you scoot UP, if that's not too big of an inconvenience for you?*

These bizarre prenatal visits seem like enough weirdness, but there is a need for gestation education; in the 1980s, it was called the Lamaze classes. They don't call it that anymore; it's now called childbirth classes. These classes are more for the dads than the moms. Dads don't really want to know anything about what is going to happen. If they could vote on it, most of them would choose to return to the 1950s when they got to stay out in the waiting area and prepare for childbirth by purchasing cigars to give out afterward, pacing back and forth and rubbing their foreheads in a concerned manner. Women, however, *want* to know all about the birth process. We are the people buying and reading *What to Expect When You're Expecting.* We are Googling childbirth, talking to friends, stocking up on anecdotal tidbits in case our labor is like any of our friends' experiences. When we are at our own baby showers, we are listening with rapt attention to every detail of the stories about labor and delivery from our friends and family.

At the Lamaze classes I went to, they made us watch films. The people who make these childbirth films seemed somehow convinced that if they showed footage of all the details of birth, we would come away enraptured by the miracle of new life. In reality, these films were a weird science hybrid of those you'd see in biology class and the ones they'd make you watch in Driver's Ed—fascinating and disturbing. I think that's the first time most men get a clue about what is going to happen to their woman, and frankly, they *really* do *not* want to know. But they also now know they are somehow expected to overcome the urge to flee (inspired by images they have just seen) and fulfill their destiny by become great birthing partners.

This is a relatively new development in civilization. For thousands of years women tended to other women during the labor and delivery of babies. Men waited outside. For them childbirth was a womanly mystery, and men liked birthing like that. I believe that one day there was a secret summit of the women of the world, and they concluded, "This is not fair. If we've got to suffer to bring offspring into the world, the very least men can do is be there and watch us do this heroic thing." But men wouldn't be there and watch unless they could be convinced that they were needed there. So women had to think up a job for the man during labor and delivery. Unfortunately, the best they came up with was: Feed us ice chips and distract us with baseball-like chatter, "Breathe, honey. Focus, honey. Breathe, that's right; that was a good one. Good work, honey. Hey, batter, batter."

Lamaze must be French for "give him something to do." My husband, John, *did* all the approved Lamaze phrases during the birth of our first child. In fact, there was a point where I told him that he might be *over*achieving in the massaging and talking area; he was so nervous that he practically rubbed a hole in my hand. For the second baby, he decided the talking part might be overrated; he just patted my hand empathetically and got the nurse when I needed her. By the time we got to baby number three, John sat in the room reading the newspaper and watching TV until it was time for me to push. Still, I was glad he was there for all three births, if for no other reason than it was a persuasive argument in favor of the doctor's note, which forbade anything south of the equator for a good six weeks.

During labor, there is a portion called "transition." This is when the baby is moving into the birth canal and stuff starts happening a little faster. In one Lamaze session they warn the men that the mom-to-be might become agitated during this phase and say things to him that are not very nice. This is to be expected, the professionals say, and the mom doesn't really mean the awful things she is saying.

I have come to believe that this phase is actually the culmination of the aggravation from those prenatal visits backing up on the woman; she needs to vent about all that has happened so that she can rid herself of a ton of negativity before her innocent baby comes into this world. *That* and the fact that she is totally done having a Volkswagen Beetle–size being parked inside of her. "Transition" is the time during which a woman works up enough frustration steam to push the VW Bug outta there.

If you are the woman in labor, you morph into an amateur contortionist. The labor and delivery nurse tells you, "Now, Ms. Renfroe, on this next contraction we want you to put your knees up next to your ears and push!" Any other time in my life, I would have told her to please lay down the crack pipe, but I was always *so ready* to have the child by that point that I would literally try any ridiculous thing the nurse suggested.

"And push," she'd say. "And just one more push. That was a really good one. Let's have one more push. And another one. Good. Just one more." This is a lie that can go on for hours, this "one more" deception. I have no idea why they think you actually believe them when they've been saying the same phrases over and over unless epidurals affect your short-term memory. You try to block out the nurse and the doctor and birthing coach (whoever it may be) "just one more-ing." Then, suddenly, it's out! It's yours! It's crying! And the relief you feel at hearing that child cry is indescribable. Unfortunately, this is probably the *last* time you will feel relief when you hear that wail.

For one moment, though, you feel pure joy.

At least that's how childbirth happened for me. I know some women have Cesarean sections, some have peaceful epidurals with a couple of pushes, and some adopt and skip the whole thing (they pant, blow, and push their way through mountains of paperwork instead). But for me, getting three little Renfroes into the world was an effort of epic proportions. And that was just to get them up to sunlight.

By the way, babies don't really look like those Gerber ads for the first couple of days, but if you think of where they came from and how they got out, it's amazing they look as good as they do. People are generally kind and refrain from saying things like "What a pointy head!" or "Do you think his little ears will eventually even out?" And right after the baby has made its appearance in the world, you get a small window of respite wherein he sleeps a lot for about the same amount of time as your HMO will let you stay in the hospital. I have no idea how the babies know how long that is, but they generally start waking up and creating inordinate amounts of decibels about the time you take them home. This is usually the first time a new mother suspects that she may have been sent home from the hospital with the wrong baby.

With my first baby I asked the lactation nurse, "How will I know when my milk has come in?" She just nodded and smiled and said, "Oh, honey, you'll know." I kept thinking, *How? How will I know? This is my first . . . surely there's some better answer than "You'll know." She said that my milk will "come in"—does that mean it is somewhere on back order? Is it on the truck ready for a schedule delivery? If I fall asleep, will I miss the visit from the Lactation Fairy?* But she was right. On the second day after I gave birth, I was awakened by the vague knowledge that there were Dolly Parton–worthy boulders sitting where my Mary Lou Retton breasts had been. This was a stunning and painful development: I had enough milk to feed my newborn and (obviously) several others. It was also helpful to have these gargantuan boulders to offset the complete loss of a waistline. It *almost* balanced things out.

Any woman who has breast-fed can tell you that your body has something called your "let-down reflex." This is why lactating females must have some sort of shield or padding in their bras at all times. For the first week or so I used the shields that they tell you are made for your lactating needs. They're round, they're soft, they cost money, and they have to be washed. Plus they also hold less than an ounce of milk before they start leaking. I was an overachieving lactator. I produced an ounce in the first nanosecond that my milk let down. Fortunately, I discovered Viva paper towels (soft, strong, absorbent, affordable, disposable!). If you fold two of them into quarters, you can absorb half the Ohio River if need be. These squares folded and inserted into your bra look really silly under normal clothing, but at this time of your life you don't have a wardrobe for this no-man's-land. You are not wearing maternity but you're nowhere near anything prepregnancy. I was rocking the husband's shirts (which unbutton nicely for breast-feeding) and hospital scrub pants (drawstrings). This was fine, since my social calendar wasn't really hoppin' at the time.

I can remember getting stir-crazy about Day Four and going to the grocery store while baby was napping with The Dad Unit—and hearing someone else's baby cry over on Aisle Seven. It did not matter that this was not my child. This was A Child

That I Was Capable of Feeding. My brain told my breasts that this was a DefCon 4 situation, and even before I could try to divert my mind with other thoughts (What are the state capitals? What is my mother's Social Security number? What is the square root of pi?), I began to soak through my trusty Viva square. This was yet another clue that I was no longer in total control of my life. Something beyond my reason was driving this train.

In retrospect, I see that this is the message from the moment the EPT stick shows a plus sign: responsibility without control. Welcome to motherhood.

Without a Manual

(Or, Why Do They Let You Take These Things Home Without One?)

When you are a new mom, you are fiercely conflicted about your mothering skills. On the one hand you want to do nothing but care for and live up to the awe-inspiring responsibility that has just been handed to you, wrapped in a cottony blanket and still sporting that hospital ID bracelet; on the other hand, there is a part of your brain that whispers, "If you start now, you might make the border by sunup." On the one hand, you have absolutely no idea what you are doing; on the other hand, you feel that no one else on earth could ever do it any better.

When I had my first baby, I knew that I was going to hold him wrong or let his head flop back or do something that would damage him forever. I was a bundle of insecurities—until my mother-in-law came into the hospital room. My mother-in-law is a fine woman who has had plenty of experience with babies. She didn't do anything *wrong* with my baby; she was just holding him. But I felt this overwhelming urge to rip him from her arms. This emotion was completely groundless and bizarre, yet so strong. I was experiencing the internal conflict I like to call Novice/Expert Motherhood Syndrome: the deep knowledge that you don't know what you're doing *better* than anyone else.

This is the feeling that drives us to read parenting columns, listen to parenting radio shows, buy books on parenting, ask everyone's advice on parenting, surf parenting Web sites, commit chapter and verse of every parenting book to memory, and go to any and every parenting seminar. We somehow believe that knowledge is power, and that is partly true. Parenting experts can give us general guidelines about the behavioral tendencies and developmental markers that pertain to children in certain age ranges. They can suggest skills we can use to handle certain conflicts and crises. They can tell us what certain physical symptoms may indicate. They can point us to other experts in more specialized areas. What they cannot do, however, is give us the two things we need most when we're parenting: the ability to relax and enjoy our children, and the confidence to trust our intuition. The only thing that provides that? Experience.

All those books and magazines and radio programs and seminars should have the itty-bitty fine print that comes on every diet pill ad: "Actual results may vary."

Remember, motherhood doesn't involve any sort of certification. You must be certified to drive a car, be a lifeguard, open a hot dog stand, administer CPR, or go fishing, but you are freely permitted to give birth and raise a child from scratch. No kind of license or training required. Apparently anyone with ovaries and a willing partner, petri dish, surrogate, or adoption agency can have a child. Society just throws you in the deep end of the pool and stands on the side, waving and smiling and saying, "You're gonna do just fine!"

When we left the hospital with our firstborn, we were given a week's supply of diapers and formula and a nose syringe. That was it. This was the extent of the "You Are Now Parents" kit. It seemed that the most important thing about motherhood had to do with plugging up the mouth hole, unplugging the nose hole, and keeping things clean and dry down south. I was hoping for some sort of manual for the feeding, care, and training of this little human being, but the discharge papers only had instructions for me (that doctor's note about avoiding south of the border involvements).

As we were driving away from the hospital, I was overcome with panic. A thousand what-ifs raced through my hormonal brain, and not one of those what-ifs was anything I could handle. The nurses told me how to care for the navel (lots of alcohol on it 'til the little stump falls off) but not how to tell if Calvin was really sick and needed a doctor's attention. I was given the ultimate nonanswer: "You'll know." I wished I had figured out a way to stay at the hospital a little longer so I could ask qualified medical professionals the important questions. I tried. I moved from room to room and pretended I was a different person, but they kept checking the blasted wristband. My HMO said it was time to go home. I was in the deep end; it was time to swim.

So, as a first-time mom, I started reading everything I could get my hands on in the mistaken belief that I would eventually have all the bases covered. What I didn't know was that many of the "experts" disagreed with one another, and they all argued convincingly for their theories. Some said to hold your baby and comfort your baby as much as was physically possible. Others said that would be spoiling the baby and giving him or her too much power in the household. "Lay them down and let them cry it out and comfort themselves." I don't know how other moms did that, but I never could. What were they going to use to comfort themselves? Recent pleasant in-utero memories?

John and I looked to experts on colic treatment (windup swings versus warm baths?), the best diaper regimen (powder versus ointment? aloe wipes versus alcohol?), appropriate soothers (pacifiers versus thumbs?).

It didn't take us long to amass quite a collection of pacifiers. We had them in the diaper bag, in the car, in every room of our house, in the fridge, in drawers, on windowsills, in between the couch cushions, in the shrubbery—I mean *everywhere*. Amazingly, we could never find one when we desperately needed it. Searching for the pacifier was like our own little indoors Easter egg hunt at 3 A.M. We should have kept one in a fire extinguisher case with printing on the side that read IN CASE OF EMERGENCY, BREAK GLASS. (I have a theory about this: All the lost pacifiers are cavorting on some beach in Rio with all the single socks that disappear from the dryer.)

There was also the diaper dilemma. Because we were trying to do everything the best way we could, we started out using cloth diapers. This was back in the 1980s before Al Gore had pointed out that disposable diapers might be causing the demise of the polar ice caps. Still, I had fantasized that I would stand outdoors hanging sparkling white rectangles on a clothesline where they would wave in the breeze, like banners testifying to my motherhood superiority. I, unlike The Lesser Mothers, was devoted to wholesomeness on my baby's bottom *and* the purity of the planet. I, unlike The Lesser Mothers, was willing to sacrifice for the health of my child and the good of our environment.

I, unlike The Lesser Mothers, was tragically uninformed.

It took only one (stinkin') week of superiority and rinsing those things out in the toilet for me to realize that disposable diapers were God's gift to modern mothers. Let us take a moment of silent appreciation for Marion Donovan—a mother with small children, natch!—who in 1946 came up with the idea of "boaters," the prototype for the disposable diaper. While we're at it, let's give props to the women who came before us and did the diaper-washing routine for years. Cloth diapers may be the reason women used to be so adamant about early potty training.

Besides, the smell of ammonia from the diapers and the fumes from the diaper pail were not a part of the serene state I had envisioned when I was decorating the baby's room. I have no idea why I did all that decorating, other than I saw people on TV doing it. This was a total waste of time. None of my children ever slept or played in their rooms. They were attached to *me* the whole first year.

I also bought the whole line of reasoning that the more baby stuff you have, the better mom you are. So we had it all—crib, bassinet, layette, stroller, car seat, Pack 'n Play portable baby bed; you name it, we had it. What we soon came to realize was that when it was time to go somewhere, we had to be strapped to the top of the car, since after packing in all that "necessary" stuff, there was no room for us to ride inside the automobile. (When my children were babies, minivans hadn't been invented yet.)

I now want to share with you the barely known truth that baby furniture manufacturers hope you never find out: Little babies can sleep almost anywhere with a couple of pillows propped on either side of them so they won't roll off. (Mother's Little Secret Number 117: Most children will roll off something before they are five years old. They live.) All the great pains we took to "childproof" the house were valiant yet hardly effective. It took us a while to realize that children do not understand this concept and actually appreciate a good challenge while trying to fall down stairs/open dangerous cabinets/get electrocuted.

When we took our firstborn to get his first round of immunizations, I felt like a traitor because I was holding my precious little innocent baby while some nurse who looked like she'd just left the World Wrestling Federation's training program stuck him with a needle. As an "educated" parent, I knew it was necessary and would ultimately protect him from childhood diseases, but when you are holding your newborn while he is getting stuck, it feels like you are going against the Motherhood Geneva Conventions and may be hauled in for an indictment when your children are choosing your nursing home.

And when a mom sees her child suffer—it's just the worst, isn't it? We don't deal with that well. My first experience with this particular "responsibility without control" issue was when my firstborn had the croup. (For the uninitiated, croup is an ailment that involves the inflammation of the upper airways and a cough that sounds like a bark, sort of like the noise made by a seal, only louder and really much, much more pitiful.) As a novice mom, I reasoned that putting my croupy baby in a steamy bathroom would help him breathe. That seemed reasonable. But au contraire. The heat made the inflammation worse, which made it almost impossible for him to breathe. It was January. It was the middle of the night. My husband was out of town. I was frantic. I called a neighbor to take us to the hospital, and I bundled us up and loaded us into our (sweet) neighbor's car. Much to my surprise, within about three minutes in the cold, Calvin was breathing better. Little did I supect that cold air causes croupy breathing passages to return to normal. (That trip was also my first experience with the truth that the moment you decide that things are serious enough to warrant a trip to the doctor, germs know that you mean business and back off. This is why your child often appears symptom-free by the time you reach the doctor's office.)

WHEN YOUR KIDS are small, people will say to you: "Treasure every moment. They grow up so fast. Don't blink or you'll miss it." I think I speak for a host of women when I say—we blinked. A lot. Blinking, blinking, blinking—hoping to skip over just a *little* bit of it. As a former mother to multiple simultaneous preschoolers, let me say that some days are just like the movie *Groundhog Day*, where Bill Murray gets to live the same day over and over and over and over again. It feels like that—just the same Cheerios, the same apple juice, the same questions, the same laundry. I'm not saying that it's not wonderful, just *r-e-a-l-l-y* familiar. (Blink, blink.)

When you find yourself under the dining room table with a blanket pulled over your head for the seventeenth game of hide-and-seek *today*, and you wonder, *Who are these little people and why do they think I'm responsible for them?* Then one of them finds you and gives you a grape-jelly kiss and you remember, *These ARE my kids.* And the thoughts of loving and cherishing them are intermixed with thoughts of, *Am I damaging them? Am I doing this thing right?* We are given a great deal of responsibility in the development of our kids, but sometimes it can cross over from "good parenting" into "my project."

So let me offer this one overall bit of reassurance to new mothers: Despite the lack of a manual for your specific model, most children come with a big wad of resilience. Also, by the time your kids can start keeping accounts on your screwups, you'll have the hang of things (at least, the whole "which-end-which-kind-of-thermometer-goes-in" sense of your child).

Because I Said So

When you are pregnant or preparing to bring a child into the world, you spend lots of time telling yourself that you are *not* going to be like your mother. Even if you have experienced a great relationship with your mom, this sense comes over you that you are going to be The One, The Mother of the Century, The Mom whose children rise up and call her "Blessed!" You are going to be there for them and be The Mom who has ancient wisdom available in relevant vernacular! You are going to make the wonder years alive for your kids! You aren't going to fall back on those trite phrases you've heard a thousand times from your mother and everyone else's mom.

And then you hear yourself say it.

And you can't quite believe it.

Somewhere around the time your baby gets upwardly mobile and starts endlessly asking you the "But why, Mom?" question, you utter the words that torpedo your finest intentions and sink your Maternal Battleship. You will *not* be the one to break the Trite Mother

Sayings Cycle, after all. Because you have just said THE MOTHER OF ALL SENSELESS SAYINGS: "Because I said so, that's why."

Soon thereafter you join in singing the Mom Song of the Ages, that river of collective mother wisdom that seems to spout irrepressibly from the mouths of moms, prefaced by (spoken or unspoken): "Let me give you just a word of advice. . . ."

Scientific studies have proven that moms are physically incapable of *not* giving advice if they believe they are in possession of a better way to think, act, or proceed. This is known as Compulsive Counsel Disorder.

A little known fact is that this disorder was DNA-encoded with Mother Eve and is impossible to eradicate. So, it doesn't matter if you were actually mothered by your own mother. *Some* mother somewhere said these things to you and they were deposited into your memory bank for the exact moment when you would need them: when you became a mother yourself.

Possibly one of the oldest mom-isms ever uttered had to do with food. Feeding is a universal, cross-cultural, primal connection between mother and child. It is Job Number One upon becoming a mom, and it remains a mother's Normal Default Mode. Whenever we find ourselves fresh out of ideas, we feed the children. We feed when the children are happy, feed when they're sad, feed when they're confused. It doesn't matter what the impetus is. Whether we need to celebrate, drown our sorrows, or have a moment of connection that involves carbohydrates, the response is the same: "Here. Eat this. You'll feel better."

In the movie *My Big Fat Greek Wedding*, the mom, a Classic Feeder, demonstrates the Normal Default Mode beautifully:

MARIA PORTOKALOS: "Ian, are you hungry?"
IAN MILLER: "Uh no, I already ate."
MARIA PORTOKALOS: "Okay, I make you something."

The very oldest utterance in the Compulsive Counsel Disorder phrase book may be "Clean your plate," which, throughout history, has often been coupled with "Lots of children in Third World countries are starving." This utterance is also known as Every Mom's World Hunger Awareness Campaign. If the mom has a visual aid of a map of the world, she may, at this moment, pull it down from its roll and use this teachable moment to show you exactly where the starving children are located. (If your mom does this today, it may also be a dead giveaway that she is a home-schooling mom.) The "cleaning of the plate" concept is crucial for mothers, mainly because it is what we have been conditioned to do: Children cry, moms feed.

Even moms who consider themselves seriously deficient in the kitchen have their own little specialties that are their secret calling card for the children. Everybody has *something* that they make better than anyone else—even if it's just triple-decker s'mores, grilled cheese sandwiches with two kinds of cheese melted just right and crispy bread, extra tangy Kool-Aid, crustless PBJs with Skippy. No real skill involved here, just the Special Mom Touch.

My nana (my mom's mom) used to make me cheese toast in the regular oven. When it got just hot enough, the whole slice of cheese would get a big bubble underneath it, and Nana would burn the edges just a tad to make them extra crisp. She also made the most amazing garlic dill pickles from the cucumbers and dill of her very own garden. My mom has a way with roast beef, green beans, and rolls. There is nothing quite like opening the front door of the house and having that smell of a roast in the oven and fluffy yeast rolls and gravy hit you square in the nostrils . . . and while I'm at it, a glass of big ol' sweet iced tea—which brings me to an issue that squarely divides this country more than politics: whether you can sweeten iced tea in a glass. By the way, you can't. You can put sugar into the glass and make a tea-glass snow globe, but any southern woman worth her salt (or sugar, as the case may be) knows that you can only sweeten iced tea when the tea is hot in the pot. Otherwise, you will just have an unsweetened glass of tea with a bunch of sugar in the bottom. This is what makes southerners livid when we ask the waitstaff if they have sweet tea and they reply, "No, but you can sweeten it in the glass with the sugar you see in the packets on the table." You might as well have said, "I am a northerner and entirely ignorant of the rules of chemistry, which dictate that this sugar will nowise melt in a glass of tea that has ice cubes floating in it." But I digress.

The scent of Mom's gravy announces, "Come in! Park your feet under the table and ingest my love!"

Our whole family knows that absolutely *nobody* trumps my strawberry shortcake. And each of my kids has a special here's-how-I-know-Mom-loves-me special request: Calvin loves beef stroganoff. Austin likes a pot of chili so he can make Frito Chili Pie. And if Elyse is needing a little food therapy, I stir up my Chocolate Gravy and pop some Pillsbury Crescent Rolls in the oven. If you swim one of those flaky rolls in a bowl of chocolate gravy (yes, chocolate + gravy will cure anything), broken hearts can mend, hurtful words can fade, PMS can subside, and the world is guaranteed to be set right upon its axis.

Moms just *know things* about food. They know that the creamy, cheesy goo of a dish of macaroni and cheese can put distance between their child and a bad day. We know that food can be medicinal. Take chicken soup, for example. Moms have known forever that it does something to fight off infection, open the sinuses, and make you feel better. Medical science is now backing up the mom knowledge by verifying that something in the chicken soup actually fights inflammation and strengthens the immune system. The scientists can't say for sure what the magic ingredient *is*, they just know it is doing the job. How did moms know this before the scientists? Because moms came before scientists. Moms told the scientists what was what before the scientists knew they needed to verify what their mothers told them.

Soon scientists will be able to corroborate that you actually *do* get colds from going outside with a wet head and that faces *do* freeze like that.

We are now inundated with Über Moms who are completely obsessed with everything their children eat. They have taken their Need to Feed to a new level—with lists of approved foods that must be (in their never-ending quest to make their children The Most Fit and Amazing Children Ever to Roam the Planet) strictly adhered to. These are the women who refuse to let their children attend a birthday party if cupcakes will be served. I know we are supposed to watch over our children's nutrition, but do we need to make them Cupcake Pariahs?

Traditionally, mothers want to fatten you up. You have never heard anyone compliment a new mother by saying, "Look—your baby seems to have about two percent body fat. This is way below the national average and will make for a muscular child. Great job!" No. Culturally, even anthropologically, we want to see a baby that has chubby little cheeks, a couple of chins, and double knees. In some strange way it warms our hearts to know that this baby could survive a season of food scarcity.

I don't know if we'll ever get away from the "fat baby = healthy baby" idea. But I do know that, regardless of cultural trends, moms want their children to eat. We will worry if you don't eat. We will worry if you don't eat enough. We will worry that you don't eat the right things. For moms, food is the emotional temperature gauge. If you aren't eating, something must be wrong, and if you are eating, all must be okay. Moms are emotionally sturdy and can withstand a lot, but if you want your mom in the loony bin, start rejecting food.

A classic mom statement is "Eat your vegetables." Again, medical science is now backing up Mom on this one. What Mom doesn't seem to remember from her own childhood is that many veggies have bizarre textures and fall under the category of "acquired taste."

And while we're on the subject of eating, how about this mom-ism that doesn't make sense from the get-go: "Close your mouth and eat." Any ideas on how one can eat without *opening* your mouth? Don't you have to open it to get the food in there?

Mom wisdom is not, of course, confined to food. And Mom's advice is not confined to food advice. Moms feel the necessity to comment, nag, counsel, explain, justify, spin, elaborate, defend, command, demand, advise, direct, instruct, and enlighten with or without provocation.

As we get past the food advice, further cracks and fissures and complications in the mom-child bond are revealed. To help navigate this complicated terrain, here are a few additional Compulsive Counsel Disorder gems—along with the insights into the inciting conditions behind each utterance:

"Bundle up." All mothers believe they are the arbiters of The Correct Number of Layers That Perfectly Coincides with The Dew Point/Current Temperature/Relative Humidity Vector. All moms are unlicensed meteorologists. They live and breathe to project weather patterns and what this means for your wardrobe needs right now and in the near future. But the actual phrase "bundle up" could mean any number of things: (1) Your mom has already been outside and knows that it is cold enough to make you sick, or (2) She saw the forecast this morning and thinks it's probably cold outside, or (3) She, herself, is cold.

"Make your bed." She wants to know that you are no longer in it and that you won't drop Oreo crumbs on the sheets sometime during the day. If everything is smoothed out and tucked in tight, she can assume you are no longer there and that the truant officer will not come knocking today.

"Clean your room." This is a tricky one because it's impossible to accomplish due to the fact that moms and kids will never agree on a standardized definition of the term "clean." The U.N. is looking into some sort of Global Symposium to determine if this issue can ever be satisfactorily and enforceably decided, but this is an important concept, as Mom doesn't want your future room-mate or spouse to judge her parental skills based on your lack of tidiness.

"A place for everything and everything in its place." Mom normally uses this one when you have committed a flagrant foul of not putting something back that she uses all the time (tape dispenser, electric mixer, Red Bull). This is not the time to point out that the item *was* in *a* place, just a *different* place. If you do choose to risk this defense and she looks at you with the Medusa eye, she might tell you:

"Get that hair out of your eyes." I have to say that this is a personal pet peeve of mine. They say that the eyes are the windows of the soul, and when moms are trying to peer into your soul, they really don't want to have to use their X-ray vision to get past the bangs. All moms believe that if they can look into your eyes, they can know the truth. Which leads us to the next momish saying. . . .

"Look at me when I'm talking to you." I've read in magazines that if you are walking or jogging through your neighborhood and encounter a less-than-friendly dog, the absolute worst thing you can do is make eye contact with it. Perhaps this is what kids instinctively do when moms are giving them The What For and they look away. I'm not sure what causes the looking away, but I know *for sure* that it drives moms up the ever lovin' wall. They want to lock eyes with you, so "get that hair outta your eyes AND look at me when I'm talking to you!" Ooooooo, a double.

How about one that is just physically impossible: *"Would you take a look at this dirt behind your ears?"*

Or the one that shows the level of compassion moms have for their children when they are obviously upset: *"Stop crying or I'll give you something to cry about!"* I don't know if we are trying to get them to stop crying by having them stop to ponder our baffling logic, but who can reason with that?

And then there's *"Don't use that tone of voice with me."* (Or, making even less sense: *"Don't look at me in that tone of voice."*) Moms have hair-trigger Attitude Radar, and they especially get exercised over the issue of verbal disrespect. When a mom feels that she is about to be disrespected, the hair actually goes up on the back of her neck. She get all tingly at that point and wants to give you fair warning that it doesn't really matter *what* you are about to say, since JUST THE TONE OF YOUR VOICE is enough to get you grounded for a year. It's like an early warning system so you can know when you're about ten words shy of doing something very stupid. Past this point lie only the skeletons of your former social life. This would be a prudent time to back it down a notch or two.

"Shut that door. Were you born in a barn?" It seems like this is a question that only the mom would know the answer to, but the door-shutting admonition stands. We want the door closed (to save heat, to save air-conditioning, to block the noise, save our sanity, pick one). But we want it closed properly, which leads us to . . .

"Don't slam that door!" Just close it. And by the way . . .

"Is that what you're going to wear?"

("No, Mom, I'm just doing a science experiment to see which sorts of fibers stay clean longer, I wasn't actually wearing it.")

Of course you are wearing that. It's on you already, right?

"Do as I say, not as I do." This is every parent's hope—that our children will do better than we do. It's also our way of admitting

that we're not perfect and prefer that you will excuse our moral laziness while we tell you one thing and do another. It is not our finest parental moment, and if we owned one of those Memory Nebulizers from the movie *Men in Black*, we would flash you so that you would not be able to recall any of our glaring inconsistencies. Another perennial classic that illustrates this perfectly? "If I've told you once, I've told you a thousand times—don't exaggerate!"

And then there's: *"Just be yourself."* This is what moms say when they are encouraging their kids to embrace their authenticity and originality, even their weirdness. What moms seem clueless about is that, for children of a certain age, to be authentic or original is The Kiss of Death. They don't want to stand out; they want to blend in. There will be plenty of time to "be yourself" later, because right now they just desperately want to be someone else. Anyone else. Preferably with someone else's parents.

"Use your own judgment." This is the Great Mother of All Conundrums. What it seems like you're saying is: "You think about this and decide for yourself what is right and then do it." But a more accurate interpretation would be: "You'd better think long and hard about the advice I just gave you. This gem is the result of many, many years of experience as well as the memory of painful consequences I have brought upon myself. Now, I don't want you to have to learn the same lessons the hard way. So listen up. If you choose to do something other than the course I have advised you to take, I will *not* be responsible for the outcome. And I will never let you forget it."

In other words, "Use *my* judgment."

And that leads me to a final mom-nonsense, which, given Mom's need for repetition, doesn't make *any* sense: "Don't make me tell you again."

What's amazing is that kids seem impervious to virtually all of these statements. It's as if their underdeveloped ear canals have no way to let the wisdom of these phrases get past the earwax. (This may actually be the cause of all the earaches and ear infections in small children: Wisdom Buildup in the ear canal.) But even though kids don't seem like they're listening to any of the fine advice you're offering them (FREE OF CHARGE, mind you), something kicks in around the age of twenty-one and all the irrational-yet-true things you told them finally cross the waxy canal to find a resting place in their brains. It's just a small toehold at first, but not for long.

MY DAUGHTER used to love to play Monopoly. She would have a few of her friends stay for a sleepover, and they would usually break out the Monopoly board for a game that went into the wee hours while they discussed the larger issues of life (who's cute, who's not, who's in, who's out). It's all the same stuff we talked about when we were their age, only we did it over Bugles and Tang, while they discuss it over Zone Bars and Starbucks.

My daughter and her friends loved playing that stupid board game. I never did. I just don't *get* it. Perhaps it's because I don't know anyone who is in commercial real estate, so it's hard for me to equate anything that happens on the board to anything that happens in real life. I don't get why you have those little die-cast aluminum figurines to go around the board or why you need a "get out of jail free" card. (Why are you *in* jail? What crime did you commit? It seems like you would know if you had committed an ethics violation in your business deals, right?) I don't understand the concept of "Community Chest" or why people have to pay rent just for landing on your space. I've never known if I should trust whoever is the assigned "banker" because they are over there making change right and left, and frankly, I never know if I got all the right bills back. That part slightly resembles reality.

But a monopoly of sorts is what mothers have in our heads. Mom Monopoly. Mom holds all the properties.

One of my friends' mothers was out shopping for a dress to wear to her mother's hundredth birthday. So get the picture here—my friend (in her thirties) was out shopping with *her* mother (in her early sixties) for a dress to wear to *her* mother's birthday party (yes, a hundred years old). So the mom (in her sixties) comes out of the dressing room in a very smart-looking dress. My friend says to her mom, "Wow, Mom! That dress looks great on you—I think it's the one you need," to which the mother replies, "Oh, I could never get this one. *My mom would never approve.*"

I could not believe it when my friend told me this story. I thought to myself, *When does it end? When do we stop being concerned with Mom's approval? When does the monopoly stop?*

When my kids were coming up, I had several "speeches" I would give them (every mother does, don't lie). One that got repeated at predictable intervals was the one I would give them before any of them would leave the house for any length of time (it would have to be for more than a couple of hours—like a sleepover or a youth ski trip or summer camp—something like that). In this classic speech I would remind them to respect those in authority over them, to show kindness and leadership, to stay with a buddy at all times, to treat the members of the opposite sex as they would wish someone would treat their sibling, and to remember that when they leave the house, they are representing the Renfroe name and the family of God. It was short and covered almost every eventuality without a lot of details.

After several years of getting The Speech, it got to the point where the kids could recite it verbatim. Often I would ask them, "Do you want me to give The Speech or do you want to tell it to me instead?" I figured that if they could spit it back to me, then that would just further substantiate that they knew all the provisions for which they were responsible. Sure enough, they could tell it to me word for word, and I was satisfied that they knew it well.

Fast-forward about five years, until Austin, my younger son, went off to college, I was having one of my talks with him about the responsibilities that were stretching out before him and the incredible number of things he would have to prioritize daily. He said, "Mom, you don't have to worry about this. You may not know it, but you live in my head."

I didn't know whether to celebrate that my voice was firmly established in his decision-making grid or to offer him the name of a good therapist.

Playing Favorites

(Or, As a Matter of Fact,
I Do Love Your Brother More)

*H*aving your own therapist used to mean that you were in touch, evolving, growing in your life. This was a development of the late 1950s, which blossomed in the 1960s and eventually became The Thing to Do. You were only as relevant as the number of times you could drop the words "My therapist says . . ." into everyday conversation. It was a kind of status symbol. If you had enough money, you could pay for someone to attentively listen to your problems. The less affluent had to settle for talking to each other. For free.

That kind of therapy usually includes going way back and delving into complicated issues like the way you were potty trained or if you never had a pony, and professional therapists use this information to figure out why you are having trouble moving forward with your life. These therapists insist that you are probably "stuck" somewhere in your past, and if you could just get unstuck, all would begin to fall into place in your world. This could be partly true, but maybe you are "stuck" in your past because, deep down, you really, really liked 1982. Why else would you have a mullet, parachute pants, and the boxed set of *The Bangles' Greatest Hits*?

This business of therapy became specialized over the years, and eventually you could choose from among private therapy sessions (expensive, but you get the therapist's complete attention), group therapy (where you can share your innermost thoughts with complete strangers who pretend not to judge you but are sitting there collecting evidence to prove that they aren't the craziest one in the group), shock therapy (do not try this at home), pet therapy (Fido will love you, dogs are indiscriminate by nature. Cats, not so much.), regression therapy (Premise: If they take you back to the origin of the mullet, you can let go of it and embrace a blunt cut.), and primal scream therapy (which originated in the Labor and Delivery Room, by the way). I personally swear by massage therapy, chocolate therapy, and retail therapy (preferably a combination of all three in the same afternoon).

People today don't have hunks of time to spend sifting through their past for clues to their current issues. We are now enlightened enough to know that all that digging around in the past can just drag us down and run up our bills. Besides, we all have places to go, people to see, things to do! We are hopped up on espresso and running at such a frantic pace that an hour of therapy would be indulgent. Really, it's just impossible. There's no time!

Enter the latest Nontherapy Therapy called "Life Coaching." Life Coaches don't care how you were potty trained or what traumatic things happened to you in junior high school. Well, it's not really that they *don't care*, it's more that the past is not their area of expertise. They just want to know where you want to go from here and what is stopping you. There are certification programs for Life Coaches and professional associations of Life Coaches. I'll bet there are even seminars for Life Coaches where they coach each other. These Life Coaches ask prodding questions in an effort to get you to articulate your dreams. Then they give you a weekly dose of encouragement. ("You can do it! Let's write down some action steps!") They call you at an appointed time each week to pester you until you do the thing you said you needed to do, and then you do it JUST SO THEY WILL LEAVE YOU ALONE. They will hold your hand *and* kick your posterior.

Back in the day, Life Coaching used to be called "mothering."

Moms were the Original Life Coaches. And moms really can't help it. From the time we know that we are going to have a baby, we are filled with wonderment. We wonder if it's going to be a boy or a girl. We wonder if the baby is going to be all right physically and mentally. We wonder if the music we are listening to is going to make the child smarter or if the last meal we ate is going to turn the baby against sweet potatoes. This tendency to wonder can keep us awake at night and drive us to distraction.

Perhaps the main thing moms wonder about is what their kids are going to be when they grow up. Not only do we wonder, we plan. Oh, we never admit to it (okay, so Jewish mothers do sometimes admit to it), but most of us do plan our children's lives in our heads. Moms can "guide" you early in your interests because they are the ones who initiate most of your activities when you are a kid. Here is the way Mom Math works:

Moms control the calendar + moms have wheels + moms have the power of withholding your allowance = you must participate in whatever they sign you up for.

Does it matter that you have absolutely no interest in being a ballerina? No. Mom says ballet lessons will help you with your balance and coordination. Does Mom care if you like T-ball or not? Nope. The experience will help you play well with others. Do you have any aptitude for gymnastics? Piano? No matter. Even if you're the lamest tumbler on the mat, your mom may envision you at the qualifying round for the Olympics just a few years from now. If you are a klutz on the keyboard, she still sees you taking a bow at Carnegie Hall.

My kids, who are all young adults now, wonder when John and I will ever recognize their maturity and stop giving them "input" about what they should be doing, but I tell you that years and years of Life Coaching cannot be undone at once. Little by little, moms may learn not to say EVERYTHING we are thinking ALL the time. Sometimes we bite our tongues 'til they bleed. But that doesn't mean we aren't still thinking things about what you should and shouldn't do.

If you take a look at your baby book, you can see how your mom envisioned your future. This record book holds many clues about Mom's earliest blueprint for her little angel. How were you dressed for those first pictures? Some moms put their little girls in all sorts of froufrou lacy itchy stuff, then wonder why the baby cries through the photo session. Maybe your mom dressed you in princess attire or in a cowgirl outfit. Maybe you weren't dressed at all . . . and what might THAT mean? Surely *that* find warrants a session or two of therapy.

Of course, what you might find in your baby book also depends on your birth order. You can tell which child a baby book belongs to just by looking at it. Firstborns: lots and lots of photos, photos of you inhaling and exhaling, photos of you sleeping and waking, photos of every milestone, locks of hair from your first haircut, every date of your immunizations, verbatim transcripts of what the pediatrician said at your checkup, etc. Second children: exactly half the number of photos of the firstborn and none of the extras. Third child? You're lucky if you even *have* a baby book, and you should feel greatly loved and treasured if your mom got your birth certificate stuck in there! For children whose birth order is third or higher, your mom possibly ran out of ideas for her kids' futures by then and was just concentrating on keeping everyone alive. This is why children farther down the birth order must have a lot of determination and self-motivation. The Mom Life Coach was worn down before she got to you.

If any woman ever prayed, "Dear God, I just want to be the center of someone's universe," this prayer took on whole new meanings when she had more than one child. With two or more children, you are not only the center of more than one person's universe, but you are also under a microscope: Your every move and motive is scrutinized and analyzed to determine if the love quotient you give out is equal for all. (I have a theory that several of the Founding Fathers of our country must have been middle children. Who else would work so hard to champion absolute equality?)

Whenever there was something to be split up among our kids, my husband and I adopted the "one divide, one choose" rule.

Under this construct, whatever was to be divvied up was put out and one of the kids got to split it, but the measurer had to let the nonmeasurers be the first to choose. As you can imagine, with that rule in mind, every piece of pie and every candy bar was divided with an eye to mere *millimeters*!

But as much as that procedure helped out with things like chocolate cake and the last chicken strip, it set a dangerous precedent for other areas like Christmas presents. You can try as hard as you want to spend the exact same amount on each child (some moms even get down to the penny, purchasing an extra piece of bubble gum so that everything will be "fair"), but the problem is that the *kids don't read the receipts* and they will perceive that someone else in the family is more delighted than they are with their gifts. I've tried to instill in my kids that we are shooting for equal gifting over a lifetime, not with every birthday or holiday. Sometimes it's just your year—everything you had on your Christmas wish list was on sale! Sometimes the price tag for your new set of car tires means you get tube socks and Fruit Roll-Ups. Of course this is antithetical to the spirit of the "splitter doesn't get to be first chooser" rule, but consistency in parenting is overrated.

It would be great in families if there were times when each child could get to be the "only" for a little while. When any of our kids got to be the only kid at home for a while, they turned into different people than they were in the normal mix. They relaxed about things when their Perceived Injustice Microscope was unplugged for a week or so. Unfortunately, this unplugging never lasted. The siblings came back from wherever they had been, and the hunt for evidence of favoritism resumed.

What's a mom to do? Of course you love all your children—but equally? Is that even possible? Come on, you love them *differently*, uniquely. Unfortunately no matter how carefully the affection and attention is distributed among your babies, someone is going to perceive that he or she is on the short end of the Parental Love Stick. If there's more than one child, it seems that the more melancholic-tempered one will be on the lookout for verification everywhere in his life that he is not the favorite. On the hit sitcom *Everybody Loves Raymond*, Brad Garrett's character, policeman Robert (Ray's older, *taller* brother), spent nine seasons spouting evidence that newspaper sportswriter Ray was the favored child in the family. One classic: "Everybody loves Raymond. When I go to work, people shoot at me. When Ray goes to work, people do the wave."

On any given day, you could ask any of your children to come up with a list of things that prove they are the favorite, and they might be able to come up with two or three entries if they sat and thought about it for hours. But ask them to come up with a list of things that proves any *other* child in the family is the favorite, and they could fill two legal pads, single spaced, multiple columns, in about ten minutes. Consider this the familial equivalent of Peace in the Middle East—it probably won't get solved in this generation either.

TV's Guide to Mothering

*O*We've seen some interesting mothering styles in TV-Mom Land, where the mothers rarely lose it (with the exception of *Malcolm in the Middle*'s mom, who lost it regularly). On TV, if there is a crisis, it will always be resolved in exactly twenty-two minutes. Children temporarily misbehave but are mostly charming. No one gets influenza bouts that require a cleanup by a hazmat squad, has visible teenage acne, or gets held back a year in school. Oh yeah, TV is not real. But from the media moms who have become part of our collective social psyche, our culture has taken some cues and been offered a few bizarre lessons.

LUCY RICARDO
Mom to Little Ricky; wife of Big Ricky

Lucy was the stah, dahling. I read somewhere that Vivian Vance was contractually required to stay plump in order to make Lucy look more glamorous. (I am going to tell everyone that I am contractually required to stay plump, too, in order to make my friends appear more glamorous. I'm just that kind of self-sacrificing friend.) And Lucy as a parent? There was a big buildup to the arrival of Little Ricky, but I couldn't tell if he actually lived with Lucy and Big Ricky or not. He was almost like a prop that they would drag out occasionally, and then you wouldn't see him for a few weeks. My personal belief is that Little Ricky had a secret stairway down to Fred and Ethel's place where he would camp out for weeks at a time, and Lucy was so consumed with launching her career that she never noticed. Little Ricky's main purpose for Lucy was to come out every now and again and bang on the drums for company, then off to bed (down the secret stairway to Fred and Ethel's— where Ethel would fuss over him and make him a peanut butter and jelly sandwich and he would smoke stogies with Fred). All well and good, unless Child Protective Services found out that he was living downstairs; then it would be "Lucy, you got some 'splainin' to do."

JUNE CLEAVER
Mother of Wally and the Beaver; wife of Ward

June (a big contrast to Lucy) was the woman who made every real mom feel like a slouch. She found all things domestic to be utterly fascinating and always had just-baked cookies awaiting her hungry schoolboys. She was perpetually freshly pressed and had at least one petticoat under her smart, trim skirt. She was Queen Bee of the Cleaver Clan and wielded her nifty 1950s canister vacuum cleaner with a strand of pearls and an air of satisfaction. Though television might have been new, women were not naïve. Some things are just too perfect to be anything but Hollywood.

SHIRLEY PARTRIDGE
Mom to all five of the little Partridges (in a psychedelic bus, no less): Keith, Danny, Laurie, Chris, and Tracy; widowed (it must have been either Danny's troublemaking or Keith's wardrobe budget that killed the dad)

Shirley Partridge had to be one of the coolest moms in TV-Mom Land. She not only supported her children's dreams of forming a band, but she actually seemed to believe that they could subsist on band gig pay. And they did. They were doing well enough to pay a manager. So we know this story was not real. Shirley found that she could stand back and keyboard sync (smiling all the while!) while Keith took the spotlight and Laurie played really bad tambourine.

This is a mom who might have been slightly overinvolved in her children's lives. (I mean, what teenager *wouldn't* want his mom in his band?)

CAROL BRADY
Mom to three very lovely girls, stepmom to three boys; wife of Mike

I ask you, how hard could it be to be an attentive mom if you had Alice doing all of the cooking and cleaning and flirting with the butcher *for* you? What exactly *did* Carol Brady do with her days? Normally, you saw her sitting at a table or desk flipping through a magazine or cutting something out. What was she doing? Was she a compulsive coupon clipper? Was she the original Creative Memories chick? We may not ever know for sure, but she probably had to spend much of her free time tending the flip on the bottom of her ever-changing shag haircut.

Carol did, however, point out the wisdom of hiring loyal, snappy, less attractive help instead of Lolita Nannies.

MORTICIA ADDAMS AND LILY MUNSTER
Somewhat interchangeable, as they were both monster moms, had husbands, had one of each kid, and had various weird relatives living with them

This is one of those Hollywood redundancies that make you wonder how audiences were expected to tell the shows apart. I certainly got them confused when I was growing up, but that's not saying much, as I frequently confuse my own children. Morticia and Lily were moms who saw their households as perfectly normal and worked hard to convince their children that all the *other* children's families were the strange ones. These moms put up with all manner of bizarre goings-on inside the household and still aspired to community activism in spite of the fact that they were often maligned and misunderstood. They loved their men and cared for their offspring in their own weird, goth ways— and made Halloween a more popular holiday.

OLIVIA WALTON
Mother to a really big brood; wife of John

Because I was an only child, I recall thinking of Olivia Walton as a hero whenever I was enamored with all things Large Family. I envisioned myself as a future Super Mom to my own brood of upstart writers, musicians, and scholars. The part I didn't envision was the unending state of pregnancy it takes to have a brood that large or the accompanying poverty. Reality, indeed, bites. But when I was watching *The Waltons* on Thursday evenings, it seemed that they lived in a better, simpler time. No matter that they were as poor as dirt and barely scraping by; they were a proud and close-knit clan that cared for one another and sacrificed to help each other. On any given day Mama Olivia could be encouraging John Boy to follow his dreams of becoming a writer *and* helping Elizabeth grieve over her deceased tadpole. But I always felt a little sorry that she never worked up the courage to really tell Grandma off. You could cut the tension with a knife when those two were in the kitchen. Those scenes were always a race to see if the beans were going to get snapped before some*body* snapped. Didn't Grandma fall down a set of stairs in one of the episodes? Very suspicious if you ask me.

In Olivia Walton, we saw that real life is hard and messy. And wonderful. When I was a child, she was my favorite TV mom.

MARION CUNNINGHAM

Mother to Richie and Joanie, honorary mother to The Fonz, Ralph Malph, and Potsie

Happy Days mom "Mrs. C" was no fool. Though she spent a good deal of her time in the kitchen, it was primarily so that she could hear what was going on in the living room with her kids and their friends. She had definite opinions about everyone's life and was not afraid to speak her piece. Mrs. Cunningham was a constant presence and made sure that everyone stayed connected and on the right track. She saw through Fonzie's tough-guy exterior and was the only one who got away with calling him "Arthur." She wasn't even too far gone to occasionally "get frisky" with Mr. C. What a gal.

And mothers everywhere could agree on her approach: Overhearing everything the teenagers say and do is not eavesdropping, it's "attentive listening."

CAROLINE INGALLS
Mother of three girls and one boy; wife of Charles

We occasionally saw the danger and sacrifices that would mirror history, but mostly Caroline stirred pots on the woodburning stove, sewed by the lamp in her rocker (which Charles built for her by hand), and tucked in the children; we did not see her taking a morning trek to the freezing outhouse or gutting the possums that Charles killed for supper. It must have been hard for her to keep her corset cinched tightly *and* swing an ax. But Caroline was a goal-oriented mother—grittily determined to make sure that her children were safe and educated and moral. On the prairie.

When we watched her face the harsh difficulties of homesteading, we were reminded of the truth: You've got electricity and a fridge and penicillin, quit yer belly achin'.

CLAIR HUXTABLE
Mother to Sondra, Denise, Theo, Vanessa, Rudy; wife to Cliff

On *The Cosby Show*, Clair was The Mom Who Had It All: a loving, intelligent, available husband with a high-paying job; respectful kids; a great career as a lawyer; a hip brownstone in the city; and, apparently, a law practice that demanded little of her after hours. She was loving and tough with her kids and always willing to sit down and have a talk. If I were her kid, I would have run far, far away when it was talking time. Because, hey, she's a lawyer. She's gonna lead you down a line of questioning designed to entrap you; she's going to get you to admit to the crime you're accused of and, bam!, you're grounded. One of the things I most admired about her character was how she and Cliff always came up with creative discipline for their children. When Vanessa got caught sneaking an alcoholic drink at a friend's house, they sat her down in their living room and asked her to play a drinking game with her little sister, Rudy. Vanessa was horrified, as it was Rudy's turn first, but then found out that the drink was tea instead of alcohol. Point made.

Clair was a working mom who did it all, did it well—and looked good doing it.

IN ALL, TV Mom-Land set the bar a little too high. I mean, who could live up to those women? They had writers. (Couldn't you benefit from someone creating snappy comebacks and heart-felt emotional speeches to use with your kids?) They had scripted husbands and scripted children. They had the benefit of "edit." Did a scene go badly? Edit. Miss a cue? Edit. Flub a line? Edit. Unfortunately, we can't hit the "edit" button in our kids' minds. Thus, our children enshrine these moments of humanity and store them up for later use when they need an ace up their sleeve. But we also don't have to worry about whether we're going to get canceled next season. Real-life moms will always be playing in syndication somewhere.

Eating Your Young

There are untold numbers of astonishing facts you can learn from watching animal channels on TV: Polar bears sleep through labor (I'll have what she's having!), and elephants give birth to two-hundred-pound "babies" (give that elephant mom whatever the polar bear is having, too).

And if you ever watch the Animal Planet channel for more than thirty minutes, you'll notice that, in the animal kingdom, there are very distinct mothering styles. Marsupials carry their young in a pouch for a while. Mares let their colts run alongside them and try to keep up. Mother cats evenly divide their time between giving milk and giving tongue baths. Mama Bear is legendary for her protective nature and will tear up anything that threatens her cub. And here's a fascinating bit of mother info: Did you know that mama eagles anticipate their babies' leaving the nest even while they are building it?

The mama eagle adds sharp and jagged objects toward the bottom of the nest before lining it with soft things, so that as the baby eaglet gets larger and starts wearing away the soft lining, it is met with things that make the nest gradually more and more uncomfortable. This way the baby will *want* to leave. Perhaps this is why the eagle is our national symbol. We admire the way they urge their adult children to leave home.

But one of the most intriguing studies in mom behavior in the wild is that of the praying mantis. These creatures will eat their spouse after they mate and often cannot distinguish between their offspring and their prey (this is an unfortunate tendency in many families), so sometimes they eat their own offspring. Any mother with hormonal issues can see how this might be possible.

When we were growing up, we all heard the phrase "Just wait 'til you have kids of your own." This thinly veiled threat seemed designed to serve as both a warning and a nonexplanation of whatever it was we, as children, were questioning; it always left me wondering what kind of magical lightbulb would illuminate my brain upon having a child of my own. When I held my first baby in my arms, I thought, *Ah, Mom must have been talking about the love and awesome responsibility you feel when you gaze into this angel's face and know that you are entrusted with this sweet gift.* But, of course, you only get the full effect of "Just wait 'til you have kids of your own" when your kids celebrate birthday thirteen.

When you have teenagers in your house, that is when you really start to think the Praying Mantis Mom Thoughts. On the plus side, you are not alone. Others have thought such things, too. Consider these actual newspaper headlines: INCLUDE YOUR CHILDREN WHEN BAKING COOKIES and KIDS MAKE NUTRITIOUS SNACKS.

On the minus side, through some cruel Animal Planet–like dramatic scripting of human life, it is often the case that moms are entering into perimenopause about the same time that their daughters are requiring feminine protection or their sons are experiencing the first kick-in of testosterone-driven raging hormones. Note to Dear *Mother* Nature, how could this be a good plan?

One thing that is particularly annoying to moms of teenagers is how "sophisticated" and "aware" they are when they call us out on our inconsistencies. We all know how much we love *that*. My friend Stacy had a talk with her daughter concerning the daughter's overuse of The Never-Ending Eye Roll whenever Stacy was talking to her. Stacy explained how rude and disrespectful it was and that it was a bad habit that needed to stop. Her daughter agreed to try to do better. Within one week of this conversation, Stacy's own mom happened to visit, and when she left, Stacy's daughter said, "Mom, you can never talk to me again about my eye rolling because you rolled *your* eyes about a million times while Grandma was here."

Stacy told me that what flashed through her mind in that moment was, "I am so *busted*!" When your daughter is a teenager, she turns into one large hypocrisy antenna, and her sole focus in life is to spot any contradictions between what you say and what you do. It is unnerving to find out that your children have actually heard your lectures on morality and now have the vocabulary to call you out whenever you fall short of your own standards.

There's also no time in a mom's life when creativity is more at a premium.

When my three kids were all teenagers (yes, *at the same time*), I had just about had it with droning the incessant reminder to put their napkins in their laps before they started to eat their meal. So I made a rule (just another service I offer) that if you took a single bite of food before your napkin was in your lap, you had to go to another room of the house and sing "The Star-Spangled Banner" loudly enough to be heard at the dinner table. May I just say that at least one of my children is truly prepared should Major League Baseball call for a singer to open a game? My husband was in full support of this plan until he got snagged one night by the kids.

Here's another good tactic: If you are the one footing the cell phone bill for your teenager and you are tired of them not responding when *you* ring them up, borrow our "Three Strikes and You're Out" rule. This means that we (the loving, bill-paying parents) can call you one time and believe that you could be temporarily out of range or in a place where it's difficult to hear the phone. And if we call you a second time, we might be able to believe that you might still have an issue of coverage or ring tone volume. But, baby, if we call you a third time and you are not picking up that cell, we will know that you are screening your bill-paying source and will repossess your technological umbilical cord until you are able to pay your bill yourself. Tough telephone love.

By far the most effective parenting weapon in the last hundred years? The car keys. Use the Force.

Yes, when you are being challenged by your teenage daughter about your inconsistencies or are explaining for the forty-fourth time why your seventeen-year-old-son-who-thinks-he-must-be-grown-because-he-can-smell-himself needs to listen to your wisdom, you might have a couple of fleeting Praying Mantis Mom Thoughts of your own. I have found that it is helpful to get out the cute toddler pictures at this point to reidentify these adolescent creatures as your offspring.

A secret stash of chocolate doesn't hurt, either.

High Noon at the Cart Corral

Whenever I visit my doctor for a yearly checkup and he invariably asks me if I am getting any regular form of exercise, I tell him about an extreme sport I take part in weekly.

"I run the Grocery Store Games."

He raises an eyebrow and looks over the top of his glasses like that is not going to make it onto the chart. But moms know that this is competitive, repetitive, and more tiring than any trip to the Y, yet we do it several times a week without any credit for the exercise. We refer to it as "running to the store," but it is a good deal more demanding than it sounds.

For this sport you don't need any special attire. In fact the grocery store is one place where you can see the whole wardrobe continuum in one place because people are always on their way from one thing to another. They come in their casual clothes, workout wear, karate uniforms, scrubs, evening gowns, and swimsuits. Everybody needs to stop at the store, and you just don't worry about what you're wearing. Every store has that sign on the front door that says SHIRT AND SHOES REQUIRED. I've always wondered WHY NOT PANTS? This seems like it would be a bigger issue.

Before you can do well at this sport, you need to determine which category you should compete in. There is the list-makers versus the I-never-use-a-list people (they either have really great memories or they run out of stuff often). I used to try and keep the list in my head with a singsongy song, but that was back when the items were simple enough for that to work.

Sing to the tune of "Twinkle, Twinkle, Little Star":

A gallon of milk, eggs, and white bread
A little sugar, too—hey, it's all in my head!

You can't really do that nowadays because the items are too complicated. Try singing this to "Twinkle, Twinkle":

Lactose-free soy organic one percent
Free-range omega-3 vegetarian eggs
Double-fiber whole-grain crustless bread
Chemically engineered sucrose-free substituted

Part of participating in the Grocery Games is, as in all extreme sports, identifying your personal peak performance times. You have to consider when is a good time for you emotionally; because they say it's never a good idea to go to the store when you're hungry. So unless you go directly after a meal (and who does that?), you're always at the store at the wrong time. Isn't that like saying, "You should never go to the gas station unless your gas tank is already full"?

Another thing to consider if you want to play this game well is: cartology. Not like "cartography" (mapmaking) but "the study of grocery-store carts and their behaviors."

When you arrive at the grocery store, you need to decide if you like to park close to the cart corral so you can return the cart with the least amount of hassle or if you like to get a little extra exercise with your groceries. I always park close so I don't have to walk very far to return the cart at the end of the trip. (This is planning for future laziness, and I read that such mental games can stave off early-onset Alzheimer's.) But does anyone understand why we now have something called the "cart corral"? Like maybe we're in some sort of spaghetti western? Will there be a showdown at High Noon at the Cart Corral? Should I bring my SaladShooter? Does that make the guy who goes after the occasional errant cart the "Cart Whisperer"?

When you make it inside the store, you have to pick a cart. If you happen to pick the one cart that has four straight wheels, you have won the shopping-cart lottery.

My worst driving tendencies seem to come out when I'm driving my cart: I tailgate. I turn without warning. I speed and have fits of "cart rage." And this is on a good day.

There are kiddie carts now. Some of them have signs on them that say SHOPPER IN TRAINING. Is this something we are having trouble with, training them to shop? They already throw things in the carts when our backs are turned. Maybe those kiddie-cart cars should have restraining seat belts to curtail those shoppers-in-training.

Moms who shop with children should qualify for a special medal ceremony. It's hard to navigate a store with so many wonderful, sugar-filled items all by yourself, but if you are shopping with your kids, you are one brave human being.

The whole grocery store excursion makes one question the theory of evolution, because if evolution were true, wouldn't every mom have four hands and an eyeball on the back of her neck by now? If you have just one kid—not so bad. They're basically like a hood ornament for your shopping cart. If you have two kids, you still have a hand for each; it's double the work but still doable. If you have three or more kids, you should never shop during their waking hours! The kids totally outnumber you now. It's three to one, so you're gonna have to switch from man-to-man to a zone defense strategy.

To play the grocery game well, you need to be familiar with the store layout and personnel.

All stores now have specialty departments with special people there to serve your special needs. In the deli and the meat market you normally find the people who signed up for shop every year in high school: They are okay with heavy, dangerous machinery and don't mind working near large blades. Back in the bakery, you have a bunch of suspiciously happy people. (Would YOU be that happy if you had unlimited access to tubes of icing and powdered sugar?) When you get to the produce section, the people seem fairly normal, but they have a sadistic edge, right? Because they go to the back and wait for a woman who has *obviously* just come from the hair salon. When she reaches in for a bunch of radishes—BOOM—they make it rain.

And you should familiarize yourself with the other players. I've already noted the list-makers versus the nonlist-shoppers, but as you're navigating the store, you will find that the other shoppers are divided into two even more significant classes: couponers and noncouponers. The couponers believe that coupons represent found money on things you have to buy anyway and that, if you continually use them over a lifetime of shopping, you will save a bazillion dollars. The noncouponers operate on the idea that time = money; thus, all the time that they spend scanning and deciding and clipping would have been better spent in any endeavor that would create more income rather than scrimping with their current income. Coupons are great if they're for stuff you need or want, but sometimes you'll buy things you neither need nor want just because you have a coupon for it. I've got a coupon for buy-one-get-one-free diapers, and my youngest child has been potty trained for eighteen years. It's hard to throw out a perfectly good coupon, but it's even harder to get a twenty-year-old to wear Pampers. You can recognize the couponers from the way they park their carts in front of the most coveted item on the aisle so you can't get to it. And because they're busy reorganizing their coupons, they will never see you and move out of your way.

To win the Grocery Store Games, you absolutely must master the art of the checkout.

Once you have made it all the way through the store and have nabbed the stuff you need, you must navigate the most difficult leg of the contest, the little four-foot-wide corridor to the checkout stand that I affectionately call "The Gauntlet." The gauntlet is stacked and hung and racked with stuff that, up until this very moment, you didn't even know you needed: the absolutely necessary stuff we didn't know we couldn't live without. Only the strongest of shoppers can resist the magnetic pull of magazines/mints/gum/candy bars/lint roller/deck of playing cards/air freshener/sewing kit/Slinky/Binaca/prepaid phone card/transparent tape/and a key chain with a light. Let's face it—this *is* the stuff MacGyver used to save the world!

I have, on occasion, tried the self-check lane. Never successfully. I scan the item and put it in the bag and the automated voice says, "Item not placed in bag." This does not make any sense to me; do they think I am trying to scam them by scanning things that I am *not* taking home with me? That I'm buying things and leaving them at the store? Wouldn't they want me to do that so they could resell the items? The girl assigned to help-the-idiots-through-the-self-check-lane comes over and assists me in checking myself out. In defense of my dwindling self-esteem, I no longer even try to use these lanes.

But checking out is not the end of the Grocery Store Games. We end the Grocery Store Games with the Triathlon Lugging Event (from the store to the car, from the car to the house, from the counter to the pantry). By my estimation, in one round of shopping I have walked six thousand steps, bent and stretched over a hundred times, pushed a heavy cart about a quarter of a mile, and lifted fifteen bags of groceries four times each.

Mark it on my chart, Doc.

Has Anyone Seen
a Photo of My Brain
on a Milk Carton?

*I*t's good to be smart. It's good to be really smart.

Just not too smart.

I saw in the newspaper the other day that many of the people who are members of Mensa (the organization for the super-smart people) are unemployable because they are "too smart." That's right. You can't be too rich or too thin or too beautiful, but apparently there are limits on how smart you can be and still be able to make a living.

Marilyn vos Savant (could that really be her real name?) is supposedly the smartest woman in the world. She has the highest recorded IQ (228) and is married to Dr. Robert Jarvik, who invented the Jarvik-7 artificial heart. (She was at least smart enough to snag a doctor; wouldn't you like to eavesdrop on their breakfast conversations?) She writes the mental challenge column in *Parade* magazine every Sunday. It's called, not surprisingly, "Ask Marilyn." Evidently, she has figured out a way to work one day a week, and she doesn't even have to write the whole column; ordinary people send in their questions, thus writing half of Savant's column for her. Based on that fact alone, she's pretty smart! In the column, she dishes out little conundrums or solves little problems like "Can you change one letter of each of these words to make all new words?" She answers such queries as: "My wife and I won entry into a drawing for a $10,000 prize. In all, thirteen families who'd won entry arrived at the drawing. So thirteen keys—one of which would open the gate to the grand prize—were placed in a basket, and the families lined up. We believe the last family in line had the best chance, and we were in eleventh position, yet the prize was won by the family in tenth position. We never had a chance to draw a key. Which position do you think had the best chance?"

This is an actual question sent in to Marilyn vos Savant; I am not making this up.

By the way, the answer was that all positions were equal.

Are you totally kidding me? Who has time to think up this stuff? Is this what Mensas sit around talking about?

When I was growing up, I wanted to be the smartest girl in my class. I loved the classroom. I don't know if I had a slight addiction to chalk dust or to the corrugated cardboard that lined the bulletin boards, but I always loved school. I fell in love with the classroom on Day One of kindergarten, when my teacher told my mom to make sure that I never had a chance to get bored in first grade. I always assumed that was a compliment on my intelligence until it dawned on me, recently, that she was possibly commenting on my tendency to get into trouble when I was not focused. I loved school so much that I would actually fake being well when I had a fever so that my mom wouldn't make me stay home. This doesn't make sense to anyone who ever tried to stay home by faking a fever, but I was bound and determined to board that yellow bus every morning.

As much as I loved school, it was apparent that a membership in Mensa was not in my future. Where I found I could compete successfully was onstage, and that success made my myriad inadequacies bearable. During elementary school, my mom entered me into a couple of those local beauty contest things. It was innocent enough in my little hometown, pretty much just an excuse to dress up and show off your kid. The only problem was that I was—how shall I say it? Okay, I was chubby. There was not a snowball's chance that I would be in serious contention for the beauty trophy. But, baby, let me tell you, I could sing and play the piano *simultaneously*. I used to sing and play the Burt Bacharach song "I'll Never Fall in Love Again." Oh, the irony of a plump ten-year-old singing those lyrics, and how cute was it when I sang, "What do you get when you kiss a guy? You get enough germs to catch pneumonia" and inserted my own little sneeze? The judges must have made up their minds right then and there. I got the talent trophy every time. Which was good, because I never got the Little Miss Whatever sash.

When the promoters of the big beauty pageants say, "It's all about the scholarships," I always think, *Who are they kidding?* If these girls' families took all the money they spent on pageant gowns, makeup, hair, personal trainers, travel expenses, and vocal coaching, they could cold-pay their own way to college; they wouldn't need a "scholarship." It's all about the tiara, baby!

In high school I was a good student, though not what you would call "outstanding" in the usual categories. Not brainy enough to be in the National Honor Society. Not public-service-minded enough to be in the Key Club. Not athletic enough to letter. Not popular enough to run for student body president. I worked on yearbook and was a member of the Future Business Leaders of America—I even went to the state competition for the venerable FBLA. It's too bad I can't tell you anything about business principles now. Some things just do not adhere to the walls of my brain. If only I had known that you had to work on the yearbook EVERY year (hence the name "*year*book"?). That would have been an important detail to retain. This is one of those secrets they never tell you when you enter high school: If you work on the yearbook just *one* year, you're not considered loyal enough to get the recognition on senior awards day. But I'm over it. Really. (I hope you're reading this, Miss Futema.)

In college I did attempt to commit large segments of my constitutional development textbook to memory. This was back when I thought I was going to law school and would need this information at my mental beck and call in pursuit of better jurisprudence. In those days, I could regurgitate all sorts of *Somebody vs. Someone Else* and how this decision affected constitutional law. I wrote the cases on index cards, memorized them, discussed them with other law-minded students, raised my hand, and got class participation points for knowing them at the right moment. During exams, I wrote about the cases in those standard-issue college blue books and I debated the cases on the debate team, competing against other college teams on subjects such as the "penumbra rights to privacy." Today, if you held a gun to my head and asked me to bring even *one* of those cases back from the murky waters of memory, you'd just have to shoot me.

Of course, I didn't become a lawyer. Once I had my undergraduate degree, I couldn't figure out which sort of law would interest me. I wasn't excited by a lifetime of trusts and estates (divorces and wills), criminal law (defending guilty people or fighting toe to toe with those who did), corporate law (exchanging loopholes for gobs of cash), environmental or entertainment law (tree hugging or diva managing). The point of my college education seemed to be learning that I didn't want to do what I had thought I wanted to do.

We have often heard it said: "It's not what you know, it's who you know." But if you ask any fifteen-year-old trying to pass the written part of the driver's test or a seventeen-year-old nervously drumming a pencil as he stares down at an SAT test, he would tell you that is pure baloney. In that moment, no one is interested in whether or not your dad is friends with the governor. You have to show *what* you know. Your privilege to drive or your college acceptance is riding on your ability to recall the right answers. And there are many who just don't test well. We know the information and we could regurgitate it under any other circumstance, but put a bunch of questions with multiple-choice empty circles to fill in with a number-two lead pencil and our brains turn to jelly. For some an exam is a chance to prove mental prowess; for others it induces sheer terror. But whether you have feelings of inferiority or superiority, they don't accurately reflect what you *do* with what you know. What you do with what you know is the only measure of education that truly matters, in my humble opinion.

In the summer between my junior and senior years of high school I was chosen to participate in the Fredericksburg Summer Stock Theater, where *real* actors and actresses (from New York

City!) came in for the season and and mingled with bit-part local players. I got the part of Princess Number Two in the musical *The Princess and the Pea* because I could sing and had long legs.

You cannot possibly imagine how far out of my box this whole experience was. Having grown up unathletic and Baptist, I was never picked for *anything* on the basis of my legs, as I was not allowed to show them. Ever. But my parents let me perform in the Fredericksburg Summer Stock Theater, because they wanted to encourage me to do everything that was in my heart to do. And that's really all I want my kids to know: It doesn't matter if they are brainy, talented, social, athletic, or anything else. What matters is whatever is in their heart to do. We will be behind them in that pursuit, whatever it is. As long as it's legal.

There's No Place Like Home, So Thank God for Hotels

$\mathcal{N}$ovelist Thomas Wolfe told us that "you can't go home again." This is particularly true if the place where you grew up has been bulldozed over and they have built a Wal-Mart over the top of your old neighborhood. But if your old home place is still there, technically you *can* go home again. It just won't be the same as you remember it. It's like your former world gets frosted with Shrinky Dink coating, popped into the oven, and comes out looking smaller than you recall. The staircase doesn't look so tall, the trees aren't as high, the yard looks smaller. The people who inhabited your world grew up and got real jobs. Things changed and life went on. This is most evident when you have been gone quite a while.

I have not been able to go back to any of my early childhood homes. The one in which I grew up burned to the ground from an electrical fire the year after my mom remarried. My grandpa had passed away a couple of years before, and my nana was then obliged to move into town. There weren't that many photos of me as a child to begin with, but most that did exist were lost to the fire. There are a few school pictures. (Is it that school photographers take the shot for the maximum goofy-look quotient? Or are we all just that goofy-looking our whole school life? And do school photographers later end up working at the DMV?) But there are no photos of me *doing* anything. This is probably because when I was growing up, kids didn't really have to do anything. They were just kids. You know—they *played.* And no adults took pictures of *that* because film was expensive back then. If someone was going to snap a picture, you had to be doing something important, like receiving a medal from the president of the United States. We did not have team pictures from T-ball, pictures from ballet recital, or photos from spring break in Cancun. When and where I grew up, there was no such thing as T-ball or ballet lessons, and "spring break" simply meant "no school" so that we could play all day. My boy cousins would come out to the farm and spend the whole day trying to pick cockleburs off the mama cow's coat, then shimmy up trees to escape her wrath. We would throw chinaberries down from the trees and bother Nana for something to eat every twenty minutes. Not really photo op material.

There's a part of me that is very grateful for that kind of long, slow, unstructured, even unphotographed childhood. Nowadays such a thing is almost nonexistent, as everybody runs kids from activity to activity to lesson to practice to activity with no time to get bored, and with every other moment commemorated with a photo. I firmly believe that it's a *good* thing for kids to get bored. It's a marker for them on the Boredom to Exhilaration Continuum. If you are stimulated and overscheduled all the time, then how can you know what real excitement feels like? And if you're never bored as a kid, what do you have to look forward to in life? That used to be one of the main inducements to grow up, so that you could schedule exciting things for yourself and no one was going to be able to stop you.

I intentionally tried to teach my kids the value of boredom. They could choose one activity per quarter and that was it. Woe be unto the child who came to me and said, "Mom, I'm bored." I wanted my kids to know that I was not the Activity Director of the Renfroe Cruise Line, so I had a list of "Bored Chores" that were available anytime anyone could not think up a way to entertain themselves. I only had to use it once per child.

Among the few photos from my childhood, there were no photos of family vacations, either. That's because when I was growing up, we didn't have vacations. That's right. Vacations were for rich people. And we were not rich people. We went for "visits" instead. The difference between a visit and a vacation is that on a vacation, you go to a destination and enjoy the local attractions and environs. On a visit, you go to towns where relatives live and you stay with them and enjoy their house. We always went to see my Aunt Wanda because she lived in Dallas in a ritzy neighborhood and she had a pool. I cannot overemphasize how impressive that was to me as a child. Our whole hometown had one community pool, so for a person who was somehow related to me to have her own pool, well, that was just beyond, beyond.

The first time I can remember going to see my aunt and uncle I was about five years old. I had never been around a pool before, but I thought I could swim because I had seen people do it on TV. (I mean, how hard could it be?) I jumped right in and proceeded to inhale a gallon of chlorinated water. My Uncle J.B. fished me out before I expired, and he explained to me the benefits of the shallow end. Although I have no photo of that moment, I can still feel the hot humiliation on my face as I realized that things in life are much harder than they appear to be on TV.

When my mom remarried, I was the proud stepdaughter of a biologist who worked for the Department of the Interior, so we moved out to a fish hatchery for a couple of years, then to Fort Worth to live on another fish hatchery next to Carswell Air Force Base. Those were both small government-issue houses. I've never been back to either of them. We then moved to a starter home in Burleson, Texas, fully equipped with green shag carpet, avocado appliances, and a big crepe myrtle tree in the front yard. But if you want to move up the ladder as a government worker, you must be willing to relocate, so we made a big move to Virginia. Our home there was much bigger than our previous one. It was two thousand square feet! And it had a picture window that looked out on our yard, which seemed to be the length of a football field by the time it reached the street. Mind you, I was in high school at the time, so my perception should not have been so off, but about ten years later when I drove past that house, I was convinced that they had moved the road. It was just a few yards from the house to the street! What had happened to the rest of the field? Seems that bushes and grass and landscaping happened to it. And time.

YOU CAN go home again, but it's all different. It's not only time that messes with your perceptions, but it's also Mom. Nothing can prepare you for the *Twilight Zone* feeling you get as you park your car in the driveway and make your way toward the front door. As you exit your vehicle, you start out feeling like the age that is on your driver's license; you may be, say, a very independent individual who has made your way in the world and is doing quite nicely for yourself, thank you very much. You may have a nice financial portfolio, a great place of your own where you reside, and friends who love and respect you. But with every step you take between your car and the front door, you start to feel less independent, less grown up. You might as well subtract three years off the age you are for every step you take until you reach for the front door handle. When you open that door to your former digs, you have usually regressed to somewhere around fourteen years old.

I call this the Chronological Shrinking Syndrome. What is its underlying cause? You are about to be back on *her turf*. This is Mom's House, and you are now all but powerless: She has the home court advantage.

Now I'm sure that Mom doesn't *mean* to Shrinky Dink you. It just happens. This is the place where she has scolded and molded you. It's where you got lectured on a regular basis. It's the place where you made some dumb pronouncements, the same place where you tried to escape your childhood. You start falling into your old patterns of thinking and feeling, quite apart from your will. How could you possibly feel this immature again? You are stricken with the distinct feeling that whatever amount of time you agreed to stay is probably too long.

Let me hasten to say that none of this is because you don't love your mom or want to spend time with her; it's just that when you step into your childhood home, the Chronological Shrinking

Syndrome sweeps over you and compromises all the ground you have gained as an adult. Every time you turn around, there are pictures of you at stages you hoped no one would remember, much less frame. There are reminders in every nook and cranny of your awkward growing years—the acne, the bad hair, the braces. Of course your mom treasures your development at every age, but it is these Shrines to Adolescent Angst that most seriously compound your regression. And should you bring home a friend or fiancé, you will see your mom act out your episode on Mom's Biography Channel right there in your old living room. At this point you may be feeling that it should be called The Dying Room instead.

For moms, the shrines start innocently enough, with the refrigerator. This appliance is in every American home, and its obvious use is to keep the milk cold and other food items from spoiling. Before women have children, the fronts of refrigerators are used for only two things: a memo to her husband, if she has one, and the grocery list. How simple, uncluttered, and functional. Then one day this same woman comes home with a baby, and BAM! The refrigerator becomes Grand Central Station. The two magnets that worked so well become totally inadequate to keep up with the demand. There are memos on pediatrician appointments, immunization dates, types of formulas and diapers, coupons for wet wipes and apple juice, and stuck somewhere in the midst of these important notes is the seed of what will become a bumper crop—Baby's hospital picture. There's just one at first. One tiny photo of the newest member of the household. It seems so innocent. Yet contained in that one little rectangle is tremendous power—the power to overtake the entire surface of this refrigerator with kindergarten artwork, photos from T-ball teams, appointment cards, handmade holiday cards, report cards, and all manner of miscellany that eventually gets put into your Personal Effects Chest. This is because moms have no way to decide which things are worth saving and which things need to be tossed. Mom's motto: "If my baby touched it, it should be archived."

For some women this sentiment turns into an all-out addiction to scrapbooking. These are the moms who are *really prepared* for the session of sharing your history with a potential future family member. Your boyfriend or fiancé will assure you that they think it's charming to stroll with your mom down memory lane, but your innards will have a cringe fest. You will smile weakly as she is killing you softly. And should you protest in any way, you will get the Martyred Mom Look, which then obligates you to a much higher ticket Mother's Day gift.

Then there is the issue of your old room. Has your mom chosen to freeze it in time? Has she kept everything exactly as you left it? Like a little Museum to You? There are a couple of schools of thought on this subject. Some moms like to keep everything as it was to make you feel like your room is always there. Should you send an eventual grandchild to sleep over, they can soak up some ambience from your childhood. But should *you* have to sleep in a Frozen in Time room, be assured that you will only regress further emotionally.

There are also the moms who start a mental timer the moment you reach eighteen and count the days 'til the statute of limitations runs out on you occupying your space. This mom is itching to get rid of your stuff—remember all those treasures she dragged out to the garage for the annual family yard sale and you sneaked back in? Those treasures are about to be history, kiddo. Mom's got PLANS for that room, baby! There will be a massive cleaning out, redecoration, and reclamation of space. For these moms, "empty nest" is not a trauma; it's a new workout room.

There will always be reasons to go home again—family reunions, holidays, weddings, funerals, births, birthdays, celebrations—the things that tie families together. Just prepare yourself to be knocked slightly off center as you return to the mother ship.

Live long and prosper.

Fun Travel and Other Oxymorons

$\mathcal{P}$eople need to get places. And most of these people are in my way. I know there is no way that this statistically could be true, but it *feels* true. There is an entire industry built on the proposition that "travel is fun!" But travel is fun in the same way that dental work is fun. And it costs about the same amount.

When I was a stay-at-home mom (which, by the way, is an oxymoron, too, because I spent all my time running the kids to the pediatrician, to the mom's morning out—*another* oxymoron, as you are not "out" as much as "tethered nearby," since the program doesn't last long enough for you to go more than five miles from where you drop the kid off—to their friend's house to play, to their activities and lessons and the grocery store and the bank and the cleaners and the park and the church and the drugstore; there was not that much staying-at-home, as I recall it), I used to think, *Wow, wouldn't it be great to get to travel a lot? It must be so much fun to go places and see places and stay places.*

This was a mirage.

It is a great deal of fun to get to meet people in different cities and take in all the many differences in the regions of our nation, but until they perfect that *Star Trek* transporter thingy, I will be stuck with the herding masses. I know there are people who have their own private planes and don't fly commercial. And some people, like Whoopi Goldberg, opt for the tour bus and don't fly at all. But the rest of us have to navigate:

- the-prices-that-change-hourly-but-who-can-figure-out-how and we-hit-you-up-for-these-fees-for-the-same-reason-rock-stars-date-models (because we can) airline tickets
- mean-well-but-are-probably-middle-children-who-enjoy-their-power-just-a-little-too-much TSA agents
- people who somehow snuck into the plane with seven carry-on pieces stuck in one large duffel and are now strewing them about
- a hacking TB cougher in the next seat and
- no more peanuts to chew on, so we switch to gnawing cuticles, instead. Or—if the person next to you seems to be sleeping soundly—gnawing her cuticles.

Travel is unnerving because you are not in control of any part of your life. You're on the airline's schedule, at the mercy of the weather, being chauffeured at thirty-five thousand feet by someone you don't know. (And why do the pilots feel the need to tell you the altitude? Do we really need this much information? It's not like we're going to try and parachute from that height.)

Travel is expensive. I don't just mean the cost of getting a ticket or a hotel. I am referring to the amounts you rarely factor in. Tipping, for example. I always tip. I actually *like* to tip. I appreciate when people are courteous and helpful, and I feel that tipping makes the world a better place. In New York, I get to make the world much better, because I usually have to tip five people just to get from the taxi to the front desk of the hotel.

I would also like to lament the demise of the microwave in hotel rooms. This was an amenity I loved, because one could reheat takeout or warm beverages, pop some popcorn to go with the in-room movie or quick-dry my handwashables. Okay, so maybe *I*'m the reason management took the microwave out of the room. . . .

Business travel has its inconveniences, but at least you get paid for it. Vacation travel normally requires you to pay for the pain. A few years back, my husband and I, my mom and dad, and a group from our church spent three days touring Cairo, Egypt. Our first day was spent viewing the countryside and doing a little shopping. There were many things available there for "one American dollar, pretty lady," but none that I felt justified the space in my suitcase. I did get a cartouche ring that sported my three initials in hieroglyphics (they are, interestingly enough, an eagle, a mouth, and a basket; a "high-strung verbal basket case" is pretty accurate). We also kicked around the Cairo Museum of Antiquities and saw some amazing displays from King Tut's tomb. What was of great interest to me, though, was the fact that the many artifacts and sculptures that were over three thousand years old were not encased or surrounded by anything that would protect them. You could walk right up and touch them! Contrast this with the United States, where George Washington's two-hundred-year-old dentures are hermetically sealed and roped off to prevent damage.

We somehow decided that it would be a great idea to ride a camel from the tour bus area over to the pyramids. In the souvenir stores, the small stuffed camels look friendly and cute. On the brochure, the camels look large and friendly and cute. In reality, these animals smell worse than Roto-Rooter drill bits and make sounds louder and stranger than Chewbacca. They have learned their manners from human two-year-olds: They spit and they bite. Not to mention that the camel gallop makes a horse trot feel like a ride in a Cadillac.

We rode our camels across the desert sands like "Ahab the Arab" and prayed that they wouldn't whip their necks around and bite a chunk out of our ankles. I kissed the ground upon dismount. It was sandy.

Directly following the camel trauma, we were to make our way into the heart of a pyramid to see a burial chamber. We all reeked of camel and felt itchy, hot, and sandy. I don't know why I thought this would be a good idea. (It's like someone saying to you, "Hey! I know what let's do for fun! Let's go visit an ancient indoor mausoleum that has been inaccessible for years on purpose! It'll be a blast!") But my dad, my husband, and I reasoned, "We're only in Cairo once, so let's do everything in the brochure."

The opening to the first pyramid looked nonthreatening enough. It was tall and wide enough to accommodate two adults side by side, and there was no indication that inside it would be any different. What we could not know was that, a dozen yards or so inside, the entryway began to narrow significantly and started to shrink vertically. You couldn't tell exactly how far you had to go to the crypt, since the passageway only grew darker and darker, narrower and narrower.

We had gone about thirty yards into the darkness when the tunnel narrowed to the point where we were practically duck-walking. It was uncomfortable for me, but I felt especially bad for my six-foot-five husband, who was cramped up like a camel in a pet carry-on crate. I felt my heart racing, and my instincts told me to turn around and head back toward the light, but there wasn't room to turn around! When I looked back, the rectangle of sunlight seemed to be very far away. I had no choice but to go forward into the dark unknown.

Just when it seemed that I couldn't breathe at all, the narrow opening dumped us into a dark, dank chamber. The relief that washed over me to be out of that tunnel was inexpressible. But to be honest, I was expecting a room of wonders for all my labor to arrive there, but there was only a small space that included a rectangular chamber where someone dead had previously spent significant time. This was most definitely *not* worth the camel-and-tunnel journey. It would be nice if someone would rewrite the pyramid excursion brochure to read, "Camels, mean and stinky. Pyramids, a claustrophobic anticlimactic nightmare."

We also vacation a little closer to home:

When we go to a beach, I like to be *near* the beach, never *on* the beach. I don't like the sand or the salt or the sun or the sunscreen. The only way I like the beach is looking down upon it from seven stories up. From behind sliding glass doors.

And if you go on a cruise, you can never quite tell by shore excursion descriptions which ones you should sign up for. They all sound enticing—"jungle canopy tour," "horseback beach ride," "swim with the dolphins," "chase the whales." Chase the whales? Have these people watched *Free Willy* one too many times? What if the whales decide to chase you back? Anybody remember the Jonah Incident?

I loved the disclaimer on the tour sheet: "We cannot guarantee that you will see any actual whales." Ya think? As if the cruise lines had a couple of orcas on call they could just phone up from the depths to make a special appearance for the cruisers. . . .

On our cruise, we opted for the "swim and snorkel" excursion. It promised a boat ride around the rock formations out from the beach of Cabo San Lucas and a chance to view the beautiful aquatic life around them. I donned my swimsuit and cover-up and was ready for action. Now, I'm not exactly what you might term "athletic," but I was fairly sure that I could handle dog-paddling around a boat. I was a little apprehensive about the breathing through the snorkel tube, and I had to psyche myself up to breathe in, blow out, breathe in, blow out. But the boat ride out to the rocks was relaxing, and I lost my tension as we rounded the beachfront and the boat slowed down around the rocks. Our guide told us to look at the three rocks jutting out of the water and to notice the white caps on them that resemble icing on cupcakes. He informed us that those were not original to the rock but the result of years of buildup of pelican poop. Some things you would rather not know.

I guess I failed to get the full snorkel memo, because they started passing out gear by giving us the yellow life vests with a little straw attached that you blow into to inflate. The vests had a harness to wrap around your waist and a second strap that comes from the back of your waist through your legs and snaps into the front. I know this design feature was for my safety, but a wedgie was the last thing I needed to distract me from the snorkel breathing pattern.

Our guides then fitted us with fins. I had never had these on my feet in my life, so here was another point of anxiety in my snorkel experience: How do you swim with the fins? I was fully prepared to dog-paddle, but fins were a new complication. The next instruction given was to take the snorkel mask and spit into the inside of the eyepiece and smear the saliva around to prevent the glasses from fogging up. *Gross.*

Finally, we were told that the thirty-yard area between where the boat was anchored and where the rocks were jutting out of the water was where we could safely snorkel. The time had arrived to get in. I was a-fearin'. What if I couldn't do it? What if I was a snorkel loser? Would my husband ever look on me with respect again? Would the other cruisers point and snicker at me in the dining room that night? The raging insecurity made me feel thirteen all over again.

We flipped and flopped over to the stairway off the edge of the boat where our excellent adventure would begin. Our Mexican tour guides failed to mention the teensy, insignificant detail that the water was about sixty-five degrees (okay, so it was January, but we thought Mexican waters might be warmer), and as none of us had wet suits, we were immediately channeling a famous scene from the movie *Titanic.* My feet started their frog-swim pattern (it's like a combination between a dog-paddle and a reptile crawl—it's uniquely my own), but that *doesn't* really work with the fins. As my feet were furiously attempting to do their usual moves to keep me afloat, the fins seemed to have a mind of their own. The extra twenty-four inches attached to each foot were creating quite a stir in the water while doing nothing to keep me upright or moving in any desired direction. Panic set in.

Between the cold water and the uncooperative fins, I said through my chattering teeth, "John, I don't like this. I want to get back in the boat." John said to me, "Anita, you're wearing a life vest, remember? Just relax." Well, duh. Once I stopped my feet from frogging, things improved immediately. At least I lost my fear of the headline in my hometown paper: GEORGIA WOMAN DROWNS IN MEXICO. LOCALS LAUGH.

Then there was the issue of the mouthpiece. It just wasn't working for me. The salt water kept getting in it. I couldn't get the rhythm of "breathe air in, blow water out," and the boat was calling my name. Finally, John said, "Anita, just put your face in the water a little and look down." And when I did, *wow*! There were the most beautiful fish, of every color of the rainbow, in shapes and sizes that I had seen only on the Discovery Channel. And they were playing around my fins! I was hooked. Of course, I wanted to let John know that I'd seen the aquatic critters, so I opened my mouth wide to exclaim about the fish and took in one-eighth of the Mexican ocean, complete with pelican poop.

I DO LIKE MOUNTAINS, but from inside a ski chalet. My friends continue to insist that skiing is an enjoyable, even exhilarating, form of outdoor exercise. My sons took to the sport like fish to water, and John is an excellent skier. The Renfroe menfolk love schussing and plowing and moguling.

For me, being propelled by gravitational forces beyond my control that cause me to hurtle at breakneck speed on slick wooden planks while wearing foggy goggles, trying to avoid natural and unnatural obstacles with my feet and ankles firmly strapped into unmovable orthopedic boots, my torso and legs padded only by something called a "bib," carrying overgrown toothpicks for balance—that's not my idea of fun. Not that I haven't tried to ski. Au contraire. I have taken ski lessons several times. But I must have had some sort of Ski Skill Inoculation thrown in with my measles, mumps, and rubella vaccinations when I was a child, because I cannot master the supposedly simple and certainly essential art of snowplowing. Each of my four, successive pretty-boy ski instructors made it sound like any idiot could do it: "Just point your skis together and come to a gradual stop." Sounds simple enough, but my skis had their own ideas of where they would like to point.

What those pretty boys fail to mention is that if you happen to sit (read: *fall*) down on the back of your skis, you cannot "turn" them in *any* direction. At this point you become, for all intents and purposes, a sled with no steering device. This is how I spend the majority of my time on a mountain, unable to have much regard for the lives of the other skiers. (By the way, I've noted that the other skiers never take seriously your yelling at them to move until you hit them. *Then* they get all righteous on you.)

In between my spastic attempts to stand back up, I promise God all sorts of devotion and charitable works if He will just get me off the mountain. The final straw of humiliation is that all the three- and four-year-olds in the Ski Baby Clinic plow just fine. Even without poles! My paranoia goes into full swing by the time I notice them. *They're mocking me!* I think—although it's hard to assess the full intent of the facial expressions behind those pacifiers.

The ski lift is its own terror. Who thought that it would be a good idea for people to dangle over a mountain on, essentially, a couple of two-by-fours without a seat belt? And there is too much pressure associated with getting *off* the lift. If you lose your courage in the 2.5-second window of opportunity to de-lift, it is too bad, too sad for you. You have to keep going, even *higher*, and you have to screw up even *more* courage to leap off—but who can make any good decisions when suffering from altitude-induced oxygen deprivation? When I was ten, I didn't hesitate to eat snow; now, though, I don't relish the thought of making sudden, accidental face-to-snow contact with a slope. That's a level of exfoliation I may not need.

Some folks are meant to look good on the slopes. Some are meant to be the keepers of the cocoa. I know my place.

The Mystic Tan

$\mathcal{A}$ few years ago, John and I were planning our first cruise, and I was intimidated by the cruise line fun and frolic as depicted on television. It appeared from those ads that there would be only buff, bronze, and beautiful specimens of humanity occupying the high seas with me (being less than buff, goth white, and beautiful on the inside). These people had exceptionally white teeth, wore strapless and droopless dresses, and danced like they were serious contenders for *Dancing with the Stars*. Since I wasn't going to get fit in a day, learn to dance in a day, or figure out how to arrange my coconuts in a strapless dress in a day, I was left with only one part of the equation within my control. In a moment of insecurity I decided that I needed a jump start on my "cruise look" by stepping into a Mystic Tan salon to fake my way to the bronze part. It was my first foray into the car wash approach to tanning, and the perky eighteen-year-old behind the welcome desk could sense my apprehension and tension.

"Don't worry! It's quick and easy. You'll love it."

After I prepaid (smart of them), I followed Miss Perky past the tanning bed room, past the restrooms, far, far away from the front of the building. She took me back to the bronzing room, where the Mystic Tan booth loomed ominously before me, and started to give me the "quick" and "easy" instruction spiel:

"Now, Mrs. Renfroe, put this shower cap over your hair but pull it back one-quarter inch from your hairline and uncover your ears. Then use this moist towelette to remove your makeup. Take this cream and coat your fingernails and toenails individually. Make sure that you completely cover each cuticle or they will turn a darker shade of brown than the rest of your skin. When you enter the booth, turn the knob to the tan you desire and push the button to start the motor. You will have three seconds to assume the position before the mist sprays. Close your eyes and stand with your feet shoulder-length apart and slightly bend your knees. Spread your toes and fingers so that the mist can get in between them. The spray will be slightly cool, so don't be alarmed. It will spray the front of you for ten seconds and then stop. You'll have five seconds to turn around and assume the next position, which is the same as the first position with the exception that you must shield the palms of your hands by holding them in front of your belly but leaving the backside of your arms exposed to the wrists to keep the color uniform down the arm. Then the mist will spray for another ten seconds. Try not to breathe in, as it bothers some people's sinuses. Once the mist stops, exit the booth and immediately towel off, starting at your toes and working your way up the body to prevent streaking. Take the moist towelette and wipe your palms as well as in between each finger and toe individually, being careful not to touch your wrists.

Do not shower or do any athletic activities for the next four to six hours or your tan will not be uniform. Do you understand, Mrs. Renfroe?"

I nodded my head, but I secretly wished that she had handed me the picture book version.

I did all that I could remember of her instructions and stepped (nekkid except for my handy-dandy shower cap) into the Mystic Tan booth. There were more knob options than she mentioned, so I selected the ones that seemed reasonable. When I pushed the start button and assumed the position, I *was* alarmed by the temperature, which was not the "slightly cool" she had described but more like a subzero flash freeze. That booth is a testament to automation, but some evil (male) designer thought that the "spray warmer" feature was a little too much to ask.

As I finished up and got dressed, I noticed a weird smell. I thought maybe it was the tanning spray in the room, but I still smelled it while driving my car. It smelled something like old fish food mixed with antifreeze. When I got home, I asked John if he smelled it, too. He surmised that it must be me! And that the tanning chemicals must not have been a good mix with my personal body chemistry. (That was *not* in the sales pitch: "Mrs. Renfroe, you will be the color of the Coppertone girl and will smell like an opened tuna can. You're gonna love it.")

I needn't have worried about the folks on the cruise resembling those in the television commercials. According to my estimates, the median age of our cruisers was sixty-seven. There was little that was bronze. And "buff" was just the first syllable of everyone's favorite meal style. These people were not ashamed to let most of it hang out and hang over. I was enamored with the older, wrinkly women, who were free and at ease with their bodies in swimsuits, while I was constantly rearranging my sarong. I wondered if there was a way I could arrive at that state of un-self-consciousness before I got to be their ages. Nah. Not gonna happen.

(I was not nearly so impressed with the old men in Speedos poolside on the Lido Deck. In my humble opinion: If you are wearing a Speedo *and* a toupee, you, sir, are just wrong at both ends.)

Age Is Just a Number

(A Really Big Number)

*I*t happens to me every time. I run into a Walgreens or Target to get *just one item* that I saw on sale in the Sunday ad circular and I am sucked in by the health and beauty aisle. It is no accident that chain-store designers put those sections near the front door and the registers. They know it is physically impossible for a woman to resist the gravitational pull of the latest antiaging-wrinkle-fighting-collagen-plumping-smoothing-firming-toning-oil-absorbing-moisturizing-copper-infused-pore-reducing product. We may have been happier before we knew that free radical cells were being harbored by our traitorous bodies and that these terrorist cells would attack and wreak havoc on our unassuming faces. What's worse is that everything we ever ate or drank or slathered on heretofore contributed to the demise of our skin. Flashback 1979: "Pass the baby oil! Pass the Sun-In! And you're gonna have to hold that aluminum foil closer to your face if you ever expect to get that savage tan, Jill." Now, we wander the health and beauty aisles wondering what we can do about the changing landscape that is our skin. There's a lotion and potion for any area of your face or bod. And we are buying it quicker than they can think it up.

I'm particularly intrigued by the category of makeup made from "minerals"—one of the fastest growth segments of the cosmetics industry. Does it strike anyone else that this stuff is crushed-up, colored dirt? Dirt that you can apply only with super-special expensive brushes? If someone had told you twenty years ago that there was going to be a time when women would rush out to pay top dollar to put finely ground dirt on their faces (and it wasn't a mud pack treatment that you would wash off in ten minutes), wouldn't you have had a good laugh? Now, you are buying quarries of the stuff!

All of this is because we don't want to appear (gasp!) as old as we really are. Like that is The Absolute Worst Thing that can happen to us. (God forbid the number on your driver's license matches the skin you're in.) We're busy concocting declarations to convince ourselves that it's different for us now than it was for our mothers and grandmothers. "Fifty is the new thirty"; "Sixty is the new twenty," like each of us is on a personal jihad against Father Time and the ravages of free radical cells.

I admit I was a little rattled by forty. Not much, but a little. It was the small changes that got me at first. They're deceptive, like the first fissures in the dam wall. One day you wake up and discover that several of your eyebrow hairs have gone MIA. You convince yourself that it's not so bad (hey, less to tweeze!). But you lose a few more and a few more until one day, while sitting in traffic, you pull down the mirror to check your powder, and right there in broad daylight, you realize that the missing eyebrow hairs have somehow migrated south to your chin line, where they now grow translucent for six weeks before they literally turn black overnight. This is the first clue that you are truly a permanent resident of your forties. Then you wake up one morning to discover that your metabolism has suddenly stalled out, and your body, which formerly resembled a firm sculpture, has somehow devolved into a mishmash of throw pillows and cushions. You stop shopping at Victoria's Secret because everything they sell "feels itchy," you give up trying on swimsuits because you know that the lifeguards are not going to try as hard if they see you drowning. *Voilà!* You're officially middle-aged.

Forty really *is* the middle. Unless you have incredible genes and everyone in your family lives to be a hundred, you need to face the fact that forty is midlife. Some women seem to fight back with success. I saw a photograph of actress Helen Mirren, age sixty-three, sporting and doing full justice to a red bikini, and I was truly inspired. . . . I wanted to write her an e-mail and let her know how inspirational she is. But that's where the inspiration ended. I didn't start a new workout routine or anything.

The forties are also the time when you start scheduling in your annual medical checkups. This requires some serious calendaring, as the number of tests seems to increase with every year. The first test that signals you're exiting Youth-ville is the yearly Smashing of the Girls, the Mashing of the Mammaries, the annual mammogram. I certainly wish someone had given me a clue what to expect the first time I went. I was completely unprepared. I went in sans deodorant per preprocedure instructions (what a *terrible* instruction, since, God knows, if there was ever a day you *needed* some deodorant, this is definitely it . . .) to the dressing area, where they hand you a top with two ties, two slits, two holes, and zero instructions. Then you are left in this room to figure out what goes where. Being a college graduate, I reasoned that if the test was for the girls, that must be what was supposed to come out the holes. The top did not fit well in that configuration, so I cracked open the door just a hair to see if I could spy anyone out in the hall with theirs on. Hmm . . . I went with their plan.

I then sashayed myself down to the waiting area where all the women were seated with their arms folded, propping the girls up in their unsupported states. We were chatting away, but those arms never, ever uncrossed or moved. When they call your name, you go down a hall into another room where there is a ginormous piece of equipment, and a mammography tech (A mammometer? A mamician? A mammy?) asks you to step up to the behemoth, remove your top and lay your . . . um . . . "offering" up on the "altar."

Once you have placed said "offering" there, the tech will take it upon him- or herself to move your "offering" for you. This is the point in the mammogram where you are whistling while staring at the ceiling, attempting to avoid eye contact because your girls seem so vulnerable and sad at this moment, just lying up there like little, sad roasts. When they are finally in position, the tech will walk over to a little protected cubicle and spend some time clickety-clacking on a keyboard. I have no idea what they might actually be doing with all that typing, but it seems like they might be checking their e-mail or IM-ing their friends. Eventually they hit some button that starts up a motor and down from the ceiling there descends a clear, plastic Plexiglas plate that is headed toward the area that your sixth-grade gym teacher told you to protect from harmful happenings. This fires up all your innate fight-or-flight reactors and everything in you screams, *Run! Run far away! Now!* Only the knowledge that other women are back in that waiting room depending on you to emerge unscathed so that they can brave their experience (and the fact that you are firmly in the grasp of a vise grip) keeps you from acting on your instincts.

When that Plexiglas plate finally makes contact (it is clear, by the way, so you can watch—like an out-of-body experience), those babies start spreading out and spreading out right before your eyes. It's really amazing how large they appear, even if you are a tiny, tiny-boobed woman. For those of you who are ample, it starts spreading out to the edge of the plate like too much waffle mix in the waffle iron. If it comes out the side, they will have to start over and use a bigger plate.

And right when you feel a little tear forming in the corner of your eye, the tech will shut the motor down and come over to do a visual inspection before committing the moment to Kodak. This person will invariably ask you, "Is that all right?" and you just want to explode the tech's head with all the pounds per square inch that are currently bearing on your tender tatas. Instead you try in vain to recall the address to your Happy Place. (Access denied! Happy Place currently obliterated!) I love that the tech will give you the instruction to "Be very still" when everyone the least bit acquainted with this machine knows good and well that your internal motivation to NOT move so that you will NOT experience further trauma supersedes anything anyone could tell you at this moment.

What is interesting to me is that we have been led to believe that the point of the mammogram is to look for lumps, when the obvious reason must be to flatten those lumps before they have a chance to accrue mass. The two things that they won't tell you that are crucial to the successful mammogram experience are these:

1.   Schedule yours on the same day as your best friend and at the same time. This ensures that you will laugh your way through yours, knowing the same thing's happening to her in the other room, and

2.   Make sure you and your friend ride in the same car, so as soon as the mashings are over, you can go get some coffee and chocolate and those babies will fluff right back up. (This is because of the same principle as the pie with the wrinkles, see page 111. It really works. Medical science hasn't caught up with this theory yet, but give it time.)

I am currently in that no-woman's-land called "perimenopause." This term is more precise than "menopause" because, technically, menopause is only one day long. That's right. One day. It is the date exactly one year from your very last period, which means—because you were in perimenopause and you were having irregular periods—you didn't even KNOW it was your last period or you definitely would have thrown a little party. Wouldn't it be great if your body sent out a little signal, maybe like the ones on Thanksgiving turkeys (that little thing that pops out) to let you know you're done? This would cause a whole new category of parties: Cessation Celebrations. (Torch the tampons!

Mulch the Midol! Pulverize the Premarin! Let's par-tay!) Because, what's difficult isn't menopause but this perimenopause thing that comes first, which gives us all fits and turns us into a hot-flashin'-sack-of-crazy-hormones mess. From what I can tell, it's basically the reverse of everything that happened to you in puberty, except now you have the stress of adulthood, relationships, and mortgages.

The whole metabolism slowdown that happens now doesn't make much sense either. If you are having hot flashes, which increase the number of cells converting calories to heat units that erupt through your skin, *how does that not burn more calories?* And every phrase I have heard used to describe this phenomenon does not really do it justice. Most people call these "hot flashes," implying something like lightning. Yes, they come on that fast, but they do not leave quickly at all. Some call this phenomenon "power surges," which would be accurate if there was a source of this power you could reach to flip the breaker off. That is not accurate, either. In my experience, a hot flash is much more powerful than either of those—more like a nuclear core reactor meltdown. The *really* crazy thing is that you can have all the stuff of perimenopause upon you and you can still get pregnant. Now that is fundamentally just not right. I have heard of women intentionally getting pregnant in that zone of their life, and I am not here to judge, but I confess that I cannot understand it; why would anyone risk the simultaneous occurrence of a hot flash coupled with a contraction?

Completely random, I know, but I heard about a gyno in New York who has opened up something called a "Pelvic Spa." I have no idea what would be on the "menu" of services there, but

I hope there are no classes called "stretch and tone." I don't know if my pelvic region is so stressed out that it needs to seek a spa environment, but it's nice to know such a place of pelvic solace indeed exists.

Here in Atlanta we have "medi-spas" popping up like Starbucks. They are like regular day spas except that they are medically supervised and the people who work there are certified to inject you with stuff. I'm not fond enough of needles to do my own research, but I hear that you can go and have a nonsurgical lift over lunch and get rid of the little lines around your eyes and mouth in about the same time it takes to get a pedicure. You can also get shot up with Restylane or Botox to paralyze your creases, fill in your lines, and plump out your hollows. They say the "new face" of cosmetic enhancement is one of "youthful plumpness." Well, that validates what I've always said: You can be skinny and wrinkly or you can have another piece of pie and fluff out.

Medical science tells us that skin is the largest organ of the human body. It's also a road map of all you've been through in your life. Every line and crease on your body is the result of time and repetitive movement. Some of us have more signage than others.

There are certain advances in science that are making women feel better *and* worse. One is the proliferation of television programs broadcast in High Definition. HD has certainly made us aware that women whose skin had appeared perfect really wasn't that perfect after all (and that makes us feel better). When you see those wrinkles, those ginormous pores, and the crepe-y lids in HD on a fifty-inch monitor, you start to feel much, much better. It's not that I wish for celebrities' imperfections to be enlarged, it's just that the average woman has been misled (by airbrushed magazine covers and small-screen TVs) to believe that she was the only one with sags, bags, and lines. It never occurred to me until recently that somewhere in Hollywood or New York City, there were women going into various stages of apoplexy from viewing themselves in this mode, which was apparently designed to show sporting events in dizzying clarity and pollen escaping from an opening flower. Good for sports. Good for bees. Bad for women. Before I was ever on TV, I didn't give a rip. I would slather the occasional Bioré strip on my nose, use some moisturizer when I felt dry, tweeze sporadically.

Now? Honey, I hightailed it to a dermatologist and a facialist and said, "For Pete's sake, fix this already." To which the whole dermatological team laughed, which seemed like code for: "Too late, even though we'll be happy to take your money and do the best we can." Maybe the purpose of my presence on TV is to make normal women feel better about themselves. (There are worse things to do with one's life.) It has always been my personal aim to have the best laugh lines in my neighborhood. If you laugh a lot, it will show. In a good way. I'm kinda looking forward to that.

But I have also reached a time in my life when it's not unusual for me to get completely freaked out simply by looking down at my hand on the steering wheel of the car. Sometimes I see it there like it isn't really attached to me. I see the crepe-y skin that looks so thin and a couple of age spots, and I think, *Whose hand is that?* like it isn't mine. I also have this strange detached curiosity when I see how my eye skin isn't bouncing back when I use my pencil eyeliner. It's like the skin scrunches up as the pencil moves it to one side—and then it just stays there! What is up with that? It used to spring back into place immediately, but now, if I don't nudge it back, it's like it forgot where to go. Some days it makes me laugh and other days I just don't look. I'm now getting these lines around my lips. They are just appearing day to day. I was sorta aggravated about them until I thought about *why* they are there . . . not from anything I am sorry about. They are there from half a lifetime of talking, kissing, eating, pouting, kissing, whistling, singing, kissing, blowing bubble gum bubbles—and I wouldn't trade a single second of ANY of these activities just to have line-free lips.

I can recall my grandmother's dressing table having only a few items on it: her hairbrush, some Pond's cold cream, a single tube of lipstick that she used for rouge and her lips, some loose powder, and some Avon rose-scented perfume. She didn't have the benefit of rows and rows of the latest skin technology, yet her skin was soft, and I always thought she was beautiful. Maybe my new goal is that my future grandkids will think I'm old and wise and soft and wrinkly and beautiful, too.

Food Fashionistas

$\mathcal{I}$t must be difficult to date a supermodel around any holiday time. The equation looks something like this:

Holidays = food. Food + models = problems.

Professional-level problems.

Most guys would feel lucky to be dating a model, but during the Fourth of July weekend or Christmas might be a different story. Imagine if you will: You must take her to parties. Sure, she's gonna look great on your arm (as she has no lumps of any sort to ruin the design lines of the dress), but will she graciously eat Uncle Bob's ribs or Aunt Edna's cheese log? Absolutely not. And when it comes time to dance, will she? No way. Because she did not partake of the ribs or the cheese log, she has only enough energy to walk a few feet, pout, pivot, and walk back. That is what supermodels do. They excel in the pivoting. Their superbodies refuse to grow inappropriate hair. Their superfull lips make superbad words if you try to get them to eat supercaloric foods.

I, myself, am something a little different—I'm a Supper Model. If you refuse to trust a skinny cook, consider me your close confidante.

Our family has found only one food category that it cannot get into: haute cuisine. We appreciate the look of it, but if you need filling up, that ain't gonna happen with the haute stuff. I know that small, tasty, beautifully presented food is an art form in itself, but we come from southern roots. Our heritage informs us of these facts:

1. If it is sweet, salty, or fried, it's good.
2. If there's a lot of it, it's good.
3. If it's sweet, salty, fried, *and* there's a lot of it, it's perfect.
4. If it's all of the above and accompanied by a glass of sweet iced tea, it is gastronomic nirvana.

These rules are not in line with the recommendations from the American Heart Association or the FDA Food Pyramid Chart, and we don't eat like that *all* the time; it is just our standard for what constitutes "good" food.

I noticed that they recently changed the recommended servings for fruits and vegetables from five servings per day to eleven. Eleven! I had to ask a friend of mine who is a nutritionist how a person could eat eleven apples in one day. She informed me that a "serving" is a half cup of a fruit or vegetable. So I guess if I had a cup of collard greens with a cup of *corn* bread, a cup of fried green tomatoes, a cup of fried okra, and a slice of onion, I would have to eat only two apples to achieve Food Pyramid perfection. That's doable.

Because I speak and perform in different cities almost every week, my husband and I get to experience a good number of regional cuisines, and we love the variety. We have several places that we have deemed "the best" at certain things. In my humble opinion, you might want to try these:

Best pineapple shake: Carl's Frozen Custard, Fredericksburg, Virginia. This ice cream place has a line wrapped around it every evening between Valentine's and Thanksgiving.

Best fried catfish: Jerry's Catfish, Richland, Mississippi. Crispy, thin, cornmeal-coated filets, served with coleslaw, hush puppies, and sweet tea. Only a six-hour drive from Atlanta. Don't think we don't do it. Often.

Best schnitzel: The Bavarian Chef, Charlottesville, Virginia.

Best carrot-cake waffles: Paradise Cove, Malibu, California.

Best Tex-Mex: La Parilla Mexican Restaurant, Acworth, Georgia.

Best chicken salad: Friends & Company, Brandon, Mississippi. A hole-in-the-wall, but you won't get a better hot lunch plate nor friendlier chitchat. Their chicken salad has grapes and almond slivers in it. They won't give out the recipe, but I don't care, as long as they keep making it.

Best pork chop and best pie meringue: Patti's, Grand Rivers, Kentucky.

Best sweet tea: My mom's, my house, Acworth, Georgia.

Our family loves everything about a meal (other than the cleanup). We like thinking about it and questing for the right ingredients. We have well-defined opinions on whether the celery tastes better slant-sliced or cut straight across. We like the smell of food when it's in the oven. We like the anticipation of what it's gonna taste like when it comes out. We like discussing what we could have done to improve it *while we are eating it.* We like talking about how good it was after we're done. We like thinking about when we are going to have it again. We are all about the food.

Our family engages in "defensive eating": We eat to (1) ward off the threat of potential upcoming hunger, and (2) to keep someone else from eating something that we project they *may want to eat sometime in the future.*

Hence, we have some food "issues." And our cuisine-oriented idiosyncrasies tend to become more personal and strident during the holidays.

I have friends who want to try out wonderful new recipes for Thanksgiving or Christmas. They tear them out of magazines or bring them home from parties and try to convince their families that this new recipe will really knock their socks off. Can I just save you some trouble and tell you what your family will not tell you? *Nobody wants to try your new recipe.* The holidays are not the time to be experimenting. Your family wants the same stuff they've been eating for the past twenty holidays. They want comfort. They want to relive their holiday memories. Sameness is not just preferred, it's essential. If you mess with the menu, you are messing with their memories. Do not deviate, even if you *know for a fact* that this new recipe will taste better. It's tradition or mutiny, I tell you.

We have some rock-solid menu items that will not be omitted without the threat of Death to the Cooks. These include fresh fruit salad (no nuts, no coconut), pimento cheese–stuffed celery, turkey, corn bread dressing, cranberry sauce, sweet potato casserole, green bean casserole, dill dip with carrots (notice that I didn't list it the other way around, as the dip is the main course and the carrot is the delivery agent by which the dip arrives at one's lips). There must be pumpkin, apple, and pecan pies or else it is not The Holidays.

My mom's twin sister, Faye, makes a cookie that is out of this world. It is called a Date Nut Chew. I realize that the name may sound like an activity provided for head cases by a matchmaking service, but this is a deliciously irresistible cookie filled with pieces of sweet dates and crunchy pecans. We take them up to our bedrooms and hide them to protect them from less discriminating palates.

We are all foodies in our family. We have camouflaged our precious leftovers by draping them with wilted heads of romaine. We've stashed our flavored olive oils on unreachable shelves. We've buried favorite candy bars in sock drawers. We don't worry about the deep psychosis that must drive this behavior. We are not even remotely ashamed about it. Every family member has favorite foods, and if you are known for hoarding certain food items, you just might receive that as a gift. One year Austin wrapped up two boxes of Cap'n Crunch for his dad and put them under the tree. John couldn't have been happier if he had unwrapped diamond cuff links.

Real Women
Don't Fear Carbs

*I*t was all over the news for a couple of weeks—the story about how the fashion show rule-makers in Spain refused to allow abnormally thin models to sashay down the catwalks there. The Spanish Association of Fashion Designers' protest over the industry's preference for waif-thin and "heroin chic" models whose hip bones, collar-bones, and rib cages stick out like concentration camp victims was met with outrage by some designers and others. I heard several interviews with representatives from various high-profile modeling agencies saying that this was a form of discrimination against the "naturally thin" models. One of the interviewers asked the question "Instead of rapping them on the knuckles and telling them to go home, why don't we find a way to celebrate women of all sizes?" When I heard the interviewer ask that question, I almost stood up and cheered, but if I'd done that I would have toppled my ice cream bowl.

It would be enormously refreshing to see women on the runways of New York, Milan, and even Madrid who were every size number from 2 to 22, if for no other reason than just to drive the designers a little batty and force them to come up with beautiful designs for all types of women. A friend of mine who watches *Project Runway* said that in one episode the wannabe designers were "forced" to design clothing for "real women" who happened to be the moms and sisters of the designers. Some of the designers were on the verge of emotional breakdowns as they had to create something that could accommodate curves instead of hanging from a pole. (Or maybe they were breaking down because they had to design something gorgeous for their relatives. In any case . . .) I only wish my friend had called me ahead of time; I would have TiVo'd that one.

They say that the average size woman in America is a size 14. I like to think, "Who in her right mind *wants* to be *below* average?" and the more reasonable side of me asks, "If you are healthy and active, what difference does the number on the tag of your pants make?" But our culture sends out powerful, persistent messages that we should be Younger! Thinner! Sexier!, and the insanity infiltrates our heads. Unless you live in a convent or in a cave with no television, magazines, newspapers, or billboards, Younger! Thinner! Sexier! is in your face 24/7. Several years ago, I heard a fashion designer on TV say that the fashion industry is all about the clothes, not the people wearing the clothes, and the best way to highlight the clothes is to drape them over a "human hanger" rather than an actual person whose curves would "interrupt the lines of the designer of the couture." God. Forbid.

I've never been a small woman myself. I was a chubby kid in grade school (back when it was politically correct to use the word *chubby*, which implied "cute"). I despised the days we had to do the standardized fitness test in P.E., and I will never forget the sensation of hanging there, shaking, for all of five seconds during the chin-up bar test. (My husband recently informed me that I should have rested my chin on the bar and let my big ol' head hold me up. Cheap shot.)

I lost my chub when I shot up in middle school. When I was at my thinnest, in my teens, I was still a size 10. What's amazing to me now is that I actually recall fixating on the fact that my thighs *a-l-m-o-s-t* touched at the top. What a colossal waste of brain space! Here I was, as nubile as I would ever be, worrying about thighs *almost* touching. Not that they actually DID touch, just the fact that they almost did. If I could go back in time and slap my eighteen-year-old self, I would. I would tell her to snap out of it, because that's the best your thighs will ever be. You should take pictures of your thighs right now so you can remember how amazing they were! You will want to frame that image of them almost touching in their cellulite-free state some-day! (Slap, slap!) I believe that teenage girls' lack of knowledge is the reason grandmas shake their heads when teenagers are in the room.

Perhaps to alter such body-image foolishness, college organi-zations are now trying to inoculate young women with infor-mation. The Greek sorority Tri-Delts (Delta Delta Delta), or "Triple Ds" on the Atlanta Emory Campus, proclaimed a "Fat Talk Free Week" with a goal to encourage female humans of all ages to stop being so critical of their bodies and stop comparing themselves to other women as well as to waifish celebrities. Even Hollywood is starting to admit that our cultural body obsession is out of hand. I recently saw an author on an entertainment show discussing how Hollywood is embracing "normal-looking men" like Vince Vaughn and Jack Black, men with some girth. They even had a term for the "normal-looking" guys—"Flabulous." But the discussion quickly turned to the fact that there is no such designation for women in Hollywood, and no one seems to be embracing "normal-looking women." In fact, the host said you would never say that a girl was "flabulous"; you would say she's out of shape.

I'm reminded of this whole body appreciation thing being a gender-related problem whenever I catch sight of my boys admiring themselves in any mirror. They stand and stare with unabashed admiration. They flex their biceps and admire them. They flex their triceps and admire them. They turn sideways and admire their physique from another angle. It's love, love, love in the mirror. By contrast, when any of the females in my household look in the mirror, we zoom in to the worst feature and linger there and walk away with a sigh. I routinely go to the grocery store in a ponytail and not a stitch of makeup, so I wouldn't consider myself overly concerned with my looks, but it is literally physically impossible for me to pass a mirror and not look at my midsection. (By "midsection" I am referring to everything between the top of my thighs to underneath my bra line.) Why do I look at it every single time? Do I think that something mysteriously happened and it changed or shrank since the last time I looked at it ten minutes ago? Have I been doing anything about it since I last looked at it? No. But I'm irrepressibly hopeful that this mirror will be the one that makes me look middle svelte.

You can examine your midsection day and night, but it seems to be more and more difficult to figure out if you are in

The Healthy Zone than it used to be. Just a few years ago, you could look at a little chart called "Height and Weight" to decide how you were doing in terms of physical health. The old chart was straightforward: If you were ____ tall, you should weigh between ____ and ____ pounds. But now you have to figure out your body mass index (the current standard used to let us know if we are too fat or too thin), and that requires a math computation that must be on the final exam for advanced calculus majors. I am pasting in the calculation from a Web site called "Losing Weight for Health and Happiness"* because I don't even know what keystrokes one uses to type such an equation:

The BMI value can be calculated with the following formulae.

SI UNITS	IMPERIAL UNITS
$BMI = \dfrac{weight\ (kg)}{height^2\ (m)}$	$BMI = 703\ \dfrac{weight\ (lb)}{height^2\ (in)}$

(Note the spelling of the word *formulae*. That's not even American. This whole BMI measure is probably some European stuff. And why should the Europeans even care? They eat chocolate and pasta and cheese and never gain an ounce.) The BMI is defined as an individual's *body weight* divided by the square of the height, and is almost always expressed in the unit kg/m^2. (That's kilograms over meters squared. Metric sucks.)

If you're not exercising regularly, it's not because you don't have a lot of options. I am amazed at the number of health and

*www.weight-loss.routes-to-self-improvement.com/Calculate-BMI.htm

fitness programs on infomercials late at night. There's that guy with the really long blond ponytail sticking out of his baseball cap with his machine that is supposed to simulate "natural walking motion." I don't mean to be Captain Obvious here, but why not just WALK? Hello?

If you flip through basic cable between the hours of midnight and 6 A.M., you can find various Pilates instructional videos, an incredible array of bizarre equipment, and even an exercise program called a "yoga booty ballet." I wasn't aware that one could attain a "yoga booty." If you have one, please let me know if it's more serene and in tune with the universe. And in one of the airline magazines, I saw an ad for a machine that exercises your whole body in only four minutes per day. My curiosity was piqued right up until I saw the price of this contraption. Let's just say there are many, many automobiles in Beverly Hills that cost less than this machine.

Have you ever noticed that the whole subject of exercise is basically a new invention? You can hardly find anything written about it before 1940. Back then, exercise was called "life." Nobody sat around inventing things like the Thighmaster back then. In the course of going about your daily business, you burned a lot of calories just getting from point A to point B, doing things that no one had invented machines to do yet. And have you seen the people who were considered "body builders" back in the 1940s and 1950s? No steroid enhancement there, just lots of beef. Lots and lots of it.

I went to Curves for a while, and though I really enjoyed it, it didn't work for me because I travel so much, and there never seems to be a Curves in the part of town where my hotel is located. (Okay, so "enjoyed" might be a slight stretch; but it's a relatively pleasant place for us ADHD types because you only spend a few seconds on each type of equipment before the voice from above tells you to "Now change stations"; you don't have time to get bored.) But the reason I really used to love to go to Curves was to listen to the women talk to each other as they made their rounds. It was hilarious to listen to these women who were there specifically to work out and lose weight—and what, pray tell, do they talk about the whole time they're there? Food! Recipes! Not just recipes modified for diets, but all kinds of fabulous recipes. As these women were wiping off their faces with their little exercise towelettes, I would hear them exchange e-mail addresses and promise to send the recipes as soon as they got home. You can't trump human nature. After a while, I decided it probably was counterproductive to go to Curves because I was too hungry from listening to the descriptions of food. My favorite Curves location has to be the one in Destin, Florida. It is in a strip mall next to a Dippin' Dots Ice Cream shop.

Exercise and self-improvement can only fix so much. Beyond that is just acceptance. Or maybe we should go with Tyra Banks's idea. I recently watched a segment on her talk show called "Fix It or Flaunt It." Tyra found people on the street, asked them what their flaws or problems were, and right there on the spot declared that she didn't know if it should be fixed or flaunted. She had her team of stylists work on each girl, and when they appeared on camera to reveal their new look, the audience was astonished that several of the girls were now "flaunting" their formerly most unattractive feature. One girl had a very high forehead. When I say very high, think "billboard." They didn't cut some bangs to hide it, they pulled the hair high up into a barrette, curled all the hair coming down the side, and made a monument to that forehead. And it worked. The chick looked positively chic.

What a great concept: If you can't fix it, accentuate it! Go all the way with it. Instead of denying the feature you're not enamored of, maybe you should put it all the way out there and make it your signature. Or, if that's just too much of a stretch for you, you could at least try adopting this philosophy, loosely quoted and oft attributed to professional motorcycle racer Bill McKenna: "Life is not a journey to the grave with the intention of arriving safely in one pretty and well-preserved piece, but to skid across the line broadside, thoroughly used up, worn out, leaking oil, shouting, GERONIMO!"

The Hairy Truth

*N*othing, absolutely nothing, can drive a woman crazier than her hair. Not kids. Not the effects of gravity. Nothing. We choose our wardrobe and swimwear based on our current state of underarm or upper leg hairiness. Whether or not the hair on our heads is obedient determines our mood. For better or worse, the state of the hair is the state of our affairs.

And you, like me, may have wondered, Why *do* we remove our body hair? At least, why do women in North America remove body hair? The rest of the world doesn't seem to mind it. Men remove hair only from their faces (assuming that man is straight and not a swimmer in search of a faster race time), and this is, overall, perfectly acceptable, since few men can rock those ZZ Top beards convincingly. But why do women remove so much hair? In her article in the *Journal of American Culture* titled "Caucasian Female Body Hair and American Culture," Christine Hope describes how, about a hundred years ago, there was a sustained retail marketing push to brainwash otherwise content, unsuspecting women into shaving their underarm hair. (Leg hair came later. The marketers set out to conquer one body region at a time.) The aim of that first campaign was to inform women that they had a problem they didn't know was a problem: unsightly underarm hair. You see, around 1915 sleeveless dresses came to the forefront of fashion, opening up a whole new field of female vulnerability for marketers to exploit. (Can you imagine living in a time when no one shaved under her arms? Actually, you can go lots of places in the world and live in that time right now.) According to Christine Hope, that first Great Anti-Underarm-Hair Campaign began in May 1915, in *Harper's Bazaar*, with an ad that "featured a waist-up photograph of a young woman who appears to be dressed in a slip with a toga-like outfit covering one shoulder. Her arms are arched over her head, revealing perfectly clear armpits. The first part of the ad read, 'Summer Dress and Modern Dancing combine to make necessary the removal of objectionable hair.'" Dancing? This was the impetus for shaving? And was there no dancing in the summers *before* this development?

"No, Francine. We cannot dance between Memorial Day and Labor Day. Too much hair."

Within three months, Hope tells us, the once-shocking term "underarm" was widely used. (What term did people use to talk about this region before then? "The Noxious Hollows"? "The Hairy Pits of Despair"?) A few of the magazine ads mentioned hygiene as a motive for getting rid of hair, but most appealed strictly to vanity. "The Woman of Fashion says the underarm must be as smooth as the face," read a typical pitch. I believe that the first "Woman of Fashion" had a controlling interest in the Gillette Company. Anti–underarm hair ads were appearing in *McCall's* magazine by 1917, and women's razors and depilatories showed up in the Sears, Roebuck catalog in 1922, the same year that company began offering dresses with sheer sleeves. By then the underarm battle was largely won. The anti–leg hair campaign was a much tougher sell. No one was showing much leg back then. Hemlines, which had risen in the 1920s, dropped in the 1930s, and women were content to leave their leg hair alone. Still, some advertisers and fashion and beauty writers kept repeating that female leg hair was unsightly. What may have put the issue over the top was the famous World War II pinup of Betty Grable displaying her legendary and hairless legs; shaving one's legs became an act of pure patriotism.

Now we are culturally committed to hairlessness.

Not the process, just the result.

Women go to painful lengths to ensure that we are—*every-where*—as smooth as a baby's behind. We shave, wax, tweeze, laser, depilitate and . . . epilate? Yes, we epilate, with our "Epi-lady" device. The people who first named this little instrument of torture seem to have come up with the name by combining *epi*, meaning "over or on," and *lady*, meaning "a woman who is re-fined, polite, and well spoken." When I merge these words, it is clear to me that they wanted to put something "over on" a "woman." And what they seem to have put over on us is the idea that pulling our hair out by the roots will make us sexy and happy. The first version of these rotating heads of twenty-seven tiny hair harvest-ers came around in 1986. I'm not sure why anyone thought it would be a great Christmas present for his woman, but a *lot* of women got them that first year. Consequently, on Christmas night, 1986, many thousands of women were using this technological wonder for the first time. Legend has it that a collective wail went up from North America, a scream so loud that it was recorded by satellites in outer space. I recently bought one of the newer versions of the Epilady, mistakenly thinking that hair removal technology must have improved during the past twenty-five years, right? Wrong. There is only one way to pull hair out at the roots: Rip it. And there is no way to rip hair out by the roots without pain. And there is no way to remove even a small portion of a field of hair—part of a leg's worth, say—without ripping over and over and over and over. (The Epilady brochure says that you will eventually need the hair remover less often, but I don't know that any consumer has actually made it to that "eventual" stage.)

Of course, if you have a good deal of disposable income, you can have a less barbaric, highly technological hair removal, via laser. According to www.hairremovaljournal.com, it happens like this: "by producing heat in the hair, which is transferred to the hair follicle, which in turn produces inflammation, and this inflammation sends a signal to the hair follicle to go into the resting (telogen) phase."

Well, doesn't it sound like someone who works for Spin Central worded this little passage? "Resting phase"? Are they serious? As in "may it rest in peace" resting? I think what they meant to say was, "We will send a little nuke-ye-lar energy down to the root and send it to sleep with the fishes. You will not be bothered by that particular hair anymore, miss."

If only it were that simple with the hair on our heads—a simple "there or not," "accept or reject" issue. But our head hair and its color and its style and its volume and its movement and its behavioral issues require negotiations of a truly global nature.

We all know that there are interpreters at the U.N. because not everybody comes from the same place or speaks the same language. At the U.N., top-notch linguists do their part for diplomacy by making sure that everyone is hearing the same information in a language they can understand. It would be oh so helpful if we had the same sort of interpretation going on at our neighborhood hair salons. I have sat in my car in the parking lot following a hair appointment, staring into the rearview mirror in disbelief at What Just Happened on My Head and longing for someone who might have bridged the obvious gap between what I said and what my stylist/colorist heard. When I say the phrase "just a trim" and ask another nonstylist woman to show me what I might mean by that, she will—without fail, 100 percent of the time (and this was done using the most stringent scientific standards)—hold up her index finger and thumb about a quarter inch apart. This seems to be universal. Well, at least in America. I haven't really tried it in other countries. But somehow, when I say that same phrase—"trim"—to my stylist, it means that she can remove anywhere from one to seven inches.

I believe that women go through enormous grief when this happens. It is as if someone has rattled our emotional core. Maybe it's because we consider the hair on our head some sort of extension of our core selves. It is one way that people identify us, perceive us, and categorize us from something as early as our birth certificate to the required "hair color" blank on our driver's license. And hair as identity goes even deeper than that, much deeper, at least for women. This hair on the top of our head becomes either our earliest ally or our arch-nemesis. There doesn't seem to be room in between. Either you have the hair type that supports the "do de jour" or you don't. Either your mom understood why the Scout Finch bad bangs were a social networking killer in the third grade or she didn't. Either you could rock the Farrah Fawcett wings in 1978 or you couldn't. And you may have been through enough therapy to make some sort of peace with your hair, but that doesn't stop you from feeling violated when your hairstylist takes off more than you had planned. Why are we so sensitive about our hair? Do we feel that since the hair was alive within our follicles mere weeks ago, that some part of us has been lost? No. That rationale doesn't work or we would cry every time we went for a manicure.

No matter the cause, after every bad haircut, we visit each of the stages that Elisabeth Kübler-Ross outlined in her seminal work on grief. You arrive at your salon with a picture of a celebrity's hairstyle you wish to emulate. You are filled with hope for your new do and fantasize that it will literally elevate your existence. Your hairdresser stares at the photo, promptly decides that this hairdo may be the one that you want but is not the one that you need; she then formulates her evil plan to substitute her professional "better" judgment for your heart's desire. Glasses are removed, the distracting and trust-inducing chatting-up-and-confessional-time begins, hair is shampooed, colored, cut, and styled, and you are turned back around to face the mirror to enter:

STAGE ONE
SHOCK AND DENIAL

You are speechless because you are in emotional shock over how this sight *could not be further* from the photo you brought in. You wonder how your hairdresser could have gone so wrong when the picture was a clear visual aid. You mutter, "This is not happening, this is not happening . . ." followed by that internal optimist who lives within all of us weighing in, "It's not *so* bad. I bet you can do something to it when you get home." Then you slide into:

STAGE TWO
ANGER

You get up and collect your things with a solemn vow never, ever to return to this establishment. You make Scarlett O'Hara–worthy vows of how you would go naked and blind before this horrible hairdresser will get her hands on your head ever again. You write your check and almost tear through to the next one with the fierceness of your pen strokes. You smile through your gritted teeth and tell the receptionist that you will not be needing another appointment. Hrmph. You catch another glimpse of yourself in the reflection of the glass door on your way out and begin:

STAGE THREE
BARGAINING

On the way to the car you make a little deal with God:

"Okay, God. If You will make it possible for me to see no one I know or care about for the next ten days while this mess on my head settles down, I promise I will call my mother twice a week and up my donations to various charities. Deal?"

STAGE FOUR
DEPRESSION

This sets in about day three when you realize this is gonna take the whole six weeks to right itself and there is no way you will be able to avoid everyone whose opinion matters to you. Then finally you reach:

STAGE FIVE
ACCEPTANCE
Because you know that you will have to do it all again in six weeks.

By the way, if you happen to mention to your hairdresser that she just cut off six inches when you asked for a *trim*, the next time you come in and want a cut, she will, in retribution, cut off 1/100 of an inch so it will appear you did not have your hair cut at all.

Just One Good Photo Before I Die

I get to speak to women of all walks of life almost every week at female-geared events across the country. It's great to get to hear a little bit about their lives and realize that, for all the details that make us unique, we share many experiences and hopes that make us strikingly similar. In fact, I have come to the conclusion that all women want the same thing in life and it's one simple, yet surprisingly unattainable thing—just one good picture of ourselves before we die.

Finding a picture of yourself that looks the way you *think* you look is the real trick. If you're lucky, you might get one in your lifetime. That's why there's such a discrepancy in obituary photos. You know how you see one that is clearly from 1957 yet the obituary lists her death this past Monday? That's because that was The Only Picture she ever liked of herself and it was more than fifty years old. When you get The One, you hang on to it for dear life and threaten your children. ("Do NOT let that newspaper run any other picture after I'm gone, ya hear?")

When you pick up your family photos from the developer (unless you have a fancy photo printer at your house—and if you do, please don't make the rest of us feel stupid because we can't figure out how to make our photos extra glossy like you can), you probably do the same thing I do—sit out in the parking lot with the AC or heater running in your car while you flip through the stash—flipping through, flipping through—looking for just *one*, just *one* good picture. Maybe this will be the bunch that yields The One. You come across one that seems like a potential candidate, but your self-critical-loathing side kicks into overdrive and you probably look at it and say, "I can't believe I look that fat!" Then you take them home and do what 90 percent of women in this country do: put them in the picture drawer or picture box and promptly forget about them for about five years.

Unless . . .

Unless you belong to that super-elite group of women who are the few, the proud—the scrapbookers. These are the people for whom the idea of photos being disorganized or unmounted brings on stress-induced asthma. In our immediate family, we do not have scrapbooks, or even photo albums for that matter. Well, let me clarify that. We do have photo albums. They sit empty and unfulfilled in the chest that has all the loose photos in it. That's right. We have a big old steamer trunk with all our pictures in plastic bins inside it. Not only that, but with the advent of scanners at every Walgreens, we even threw away our kajillion envelopes of photo negatives. The scrapbookers are puffing on their inhalers right now at the thought of my precious family photos languishing in the basement, but I prefer to think of it as my deference to future daughters-in-law: I would not want to be so bold as to assume that my version of history is the definitive one.

Scrapbookers make the rest of us look like slugs with their cropping shears and their rickrack and their stickers and their acid-free archival papers and their laminating machines and their little bookety books. They crop people they don't like out of the pictures with their powerful cropping shears, put little conversation bubbles coming out of people's mouths with things they never actually said. In effect they are truly "creating" all-new "memories" of things that never happened, at least not the way they are relayed in their revisionist history versions. Of course, this could come in very handy when your kids are in therapy in their thirties and the therapist invites you in for a session. When he questions certain events that happened that may have scarred your child, you can drag out your scrapbook and say, "I don't have any idea what Junior could be talking about . . . just look at these pages, Doctor . . . ," and the proof would be in the rickrack-trimmed, laminated pudding. Whenever I have talked to these croppers and asked them why they do it, the most common answer is "To give to my children." I will press a little and ask, "When, exactly, do you plan on doing this?" and they will invariably answer with one of three scenarios:

1. When their kids leave home, or
2. When their kids get married, or
3. When they themselves die.

All of this seems bizarre to me, because my children have given me explicit instructions that, when any of the above events occur, they do not want a scrapbook—they want a check.

The real tragedy is that these scrappers will never have the joy of letting their pictures languish for a while. They are forever playing in their photos and thus will never know the delight of discovering that set of pictures you deemed unworthy five years ago. It's just so satisfying to take the same set of photos out, fish out the photo you thought was hideous a few years back, and discover, "Man! I was thin!"

Money Can't Buy You Love— But It Can Buy You Chocolate!

Traditional wisdom (the kind you can get in Proverbs or perhaps in a Beatles song) informs us that "money can't buy you love." Traditional wisdom also tells us that money can't buy you happiness. But I've had money and I've had no money, and I can tell you from experience that money can, indeed, buy you a more comfortable brand of misery.

There is a universal truth that some people are just going to have more money than others, so it is up to us to decide if we are going to get a number and join the marathon called The Rat Race (more money, more stuff, more money to pay for more stuff, a larger place to keep all the stuff and the money, more people to help us make and take care of the stuff and the money, more worry about losing our stuff and our money) or if we are going to sit it out, wear Birkenstocks, and eat granola. I read that Oprah (worth $2.5 billion, give or take a billion for stock value adjustments) recently told *Black Enterprise* magazine, "I don't care about money." Have you ever noticed that only rich people say that? The reason they don't care about money is because they have plenty of it. But for people who don't have it? We care. And we'd like to have enough money to explore the sensation of not caring about it.

I'll just come right out and say it: I like stuff. And you can trade money for stuff. I especially like gadgets. I'm intrigued by little pieces of technology that hold forth the promise of doing things more efficiently. We recently got a one-cup-at-a-time brewing machine because we didn't all want the same coffee or tea at the same time. It's like an iPod for hot beverage drinkers. I rationalized that it was less wasteful because we wouldn't be pouring out half a carafe of unused coffee every day, but I think I really just liked the idea of having a cup of Earl Grey tea all to myself in less than thirty seconds.

This is madness, I know. If I were financially able (and had already given away money to various causes and charities, especially anything Bono supports, because that would raise my Global Hipness Quotient, which I just wrecked by using the term "Hipness") and I had even *more* extra money lying around, I admit that I would probably get one of everything in Brookstone, Hammacher Schlemmer, and anything found in the *SkyMall* catalog on airplanes. I would. That's how much I enjoy gadgets. Last summer we ordered the wind chill fan. This is an outdoor fan that hooks up to our garden hose and sprays a mist as it blows, like the ones they use at the Summer Olympics and at theme parks. It cools the air temp down by about twenty degrees so that when I am lying out in the sun, I don't actually have to suffer any of the effects of the heat. I understand that there is a certain level of madness associated with being in the sun and not wanting to be hot, but it works for me.

But no matter how many gadgets I amass, I am painfully aware that, alas, Bill Gates will have more and cooler gadgets than I. This is because he is the richest man ever (Or is it Warren Buffett? I forget.). But Bill Gates and all his money can't buy a good haircut. Come to think of it, neither can Donald Trump. I see a trend. Maybe it's another way that God equals things out. Big money = bad hair. Which virtually guarantees that I will have good hair forever. This is because I do not understand *anything* about how finances/economy/money works. It's not because I haven't tried. And recent financial events in our nation and our world have made me feel that absolutely *n-o-b-o-d-y* else knows, either, which is both comforting and disturbing.

I get the basics: I need to exchange my dollars for goods and services, but beyond that the system is a mystery. I go to the bank. I put money in. Somehow the money goes away very quickly. I know that I am somehow responsible for this, but the outgo does have a head start on the inflow, having been sitting around for at least twenty-four hours and itching to get out into the world. I suspect that whenever new, energetic money comes in, the old money bolts, frequently knocking some of the new money back out the door along with it. Whatever the mystery, the money shuffle messes with my bank account statements. I long ago gave up trying to balance my checkbook. I do get that the input should exceed the output, but I don't understand why it falls to me to have to make sure that the statement is exactly right. (They're the bank, right? Isn't it *their job* to figure that out?) So I just go online, look at the number they have as my ending balance, and I imagine the difference between the money I put in this month versus the number of checks I think I wrote this month. If the number they say I have and the number I think I should have are less than $25 apart, I go with their number. It may be bad accounting, but it saves me a lot of time. I could sit there for countless hours looking for $25, or just pay myself $25 not to care. My sanity is worth $25 to me, and if time is money, I just saved myself some of both.

Stock market? I don't get that either. I get that you buy "stock" in a certain "market," then you're supposed to leave the stock in your account for a very long time to make more money than you could acquire through interest on a savings account. The place where all of this happens is called "Wall Street"—meaning that there is a "wall" that divides the Stock Market Savvy people and the rest of the regular people who believe that the persons on the other side of this "wall" have a clue about what needs to be done with our "stocks." This place beyond the wall is inhabited by "brokers"—obviously derived from the fact that, with a single bad day of trading, you can go "broke." As far as I can tell, playing the stock market is a weird science involving a form of nationalized legalized gambling and the Psychic Friends Network. I have also heard of studies showing that chickens pecking to choose stocks and monkeys who choose stocks often do as well as brokers. In light of the volatile markets in recent months, I recommend that we let the little animals have a shot at it. At least we could rest easier knowing that they weren't postdating transactions and skimming for chicken feed and bananas. In addition to financial advisors, many of us also have a "financial planner"—they have studied finances and equations and investment options, so they can help you reach your financial goals *by selling you life insurance and taking a percentage of your money.* This does not make sense to me. Why can't we *keep* our money instead of giving it to them so they can tell us how to make it?

Here is my own two-point, non-money-professional explanation for what happened in the stock market in 2008. I don't know if this is the whole story, but it makes sense if you don't think about it. First, the all-time peak of activity on online social networking sites seemed to coincide with the moment the finances of our nation were teetering on the brink of disaster. You see? People who were supposed to be paying attention by vetting loan applicants, making policies governing the national treasury, providing oversight to federal agencies, and adjusting prime lending rates were totally distracted by checking their Facebook status. They were too busy cyber-stalking former girlfriends from college to notice that the market was about to come crashing down on our collective national heads. I can't prove this yet, but I sense that history will bear me out.

And the second contributing factor to our collective financial bust? I lay that at the feet of the bottled water industry. Talk about siphoning off billions of dollars people could be putting into savings! These manufacturers are selling something in plastic bottles that everybody *could* have FOR FREE. Then the medical profession got into the racket, proclaiming that we needed to drink copious amounts of water. Soon, we literally could not walk five feet without a bottle in hand, lest we risk being dehydrated. How did civilization thrive before the bottled water industry? How did anyone have kidney function or clear skin? Were we perpetually dehydrated yet unaware? I remember when I was a kid we used to play outside all day in the hot Texas sun (with no wind chill fan, by the way), and we would drink out of the garden hose only three times in eight hours and we did not suffer any ill effects. We drank when we were thirsty. But we now "know" that by the time you feel thirst, you are already dehydrated. And the fear of dehydration coupled with our desire to appear as though we might break out into something sportslike at any moment made us a slave to The Water Bottle Cartel. This led to the need to frequent the bathroom more often, which led to the higher profit margins for toilet paper and hand sanitizer. It's a racket, I tell you.

One of the most interesting responses to the financial stresses of late has been the rise of the "Come Sell Your Gold" home parties. Talk about taking your Tupperware night to a whole new level. That's right, just bring Granny's brooch and your uncle's retirement-gift cuff links! We will analyze the gold content, weigh it, and pay you on the spot. This is happening at the same time the TV ads and talking heads inform us that gold is the last, best investment option. Let me get this straight: Gold is the only thing that will continue to increase in value, so get rid of it?

Please allow me to offer a simpler financial plan. Invest in chocolate. Buy bars. Lots of bars. If we do enter anything approximating a real financial depression, you will not be able to improve your mood with gold.

The Purse-uit of Happiness

I have heard men say that they just don't understand women. Like maybe we are these mysterious creatures who cannot be deciphered. Men believe there is no key, no legend to the female psyche. No way to get a read on her likes, dislikes, or issues without spending astounding amounts of time listening to her hold forth on her life and perspectives. This is a myth we like to keep alive, because we enjoy the attention, but you can actually learn just about anything you want to know about a woman by simply analyzing her purse.

Purses are central to our existence. We know this is true because if you have ever seen a woman who THINKS she has lost her purse, it is a feeling that runs a close second only to the panic you experience when you think you may have misplaced a child in a crowded shopping mall. Purses are that perfect trifecta of form, function, and fashion. We quest endlessly for The Perfect Purse, we try them on, we must bond with them. This is a strictly feminine pursuit. You never see men trying wallets on, although some of them should, since their back pockets look like they're toting a brick back there.

A woman's purse is her own private domain. It is a rare friendship that ever develops to the level where one friend allows another friend to rummage through her purse. And God forbid that any man would ever dare stick his hand in there. He will not survive the day. If I am sick and dying in one room of our house and the medicine that will save my life is in my purse in another room of the house, my husband knows to just bring me the whole purse and let me fish the medication out in my dying state. He would do this rather than risk going in himself.

Our need for purses starts young. I had my first purse around fifth grade. And I haven't been without some form of one since. Every stage of my emotional teenage experience and young adulthood could be catalogued and pretty accurately defined by the purses I carried. They held my gum, my lip gloss, my first driver's license, my notes to and from various boyfriends—the flotsam of life.

If you need to get a quick read on a woman/friend, you absolutely can do it by her choice of purse. Even if she doesn't carry one. That fact alone will tell you loads about her. Those women are normally the ones who are so righteous about their status. "I don't carry a purse, I don't really need one. . . ." If you investigate further, you will usually find that her car IS her purse, with stuff strewn all over the seats or a secret locker stashed away in the workroom. There's just no way around it—girls have stuff.

I call this take on a woman her "purse-onality." It's pretty accurate. Just do a quick survey of your friends the next time

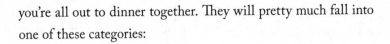

you're all out to dinner together. They will pretty much fall into one of these categories:

THE TINY TOTE-R

This woman is the one who can get the entire contents of her day into seven square inches. If this is the case, you can bet she has the control issues that go with it. This is the girl who has tight hospital corners on her bed, tight abs from perfectly controlled crunches, and a perfect credit score because she pays her bills *ahead of time.* She is most useful in your circle of friends because she has the unlimited Amex to go with the perfect credit score so you never have to worry about financing a spontaneous trip to Mexico.

THE "MORE IS BETTER"

This girl likes 'em big! The bigger the better. If they made a rolling footlocker at Dooney & Bourke, she'd buy it. This woman basically never got over carrying the diaper bag. And she is the Perpetual Girl Scout, prepared for any eventuality with a veritable plethora of items in her humongous bag. You could call her The Unofficial FDA for all the food and drugs she keeps in there. She is necessary to your group of friends because she would have everything you would need to survive for a spontaneous trip to Mexico, including swimsuits, sunscreen, and Imodium. Oh yes, it's all in there.

THE SERIAL MONOGAMIST

This is the one who buys one purse and sticks with it for twelve years. But this tendency highlights her best and worst at one whack. Her best? She's loyal. Her worst? She's cheap. She has your back at all times, unless it involves twelve cents' difference when splitting the lunch tab. If a purse is still functional, she'll hold on to it long past its prime. This means she will also not give up on you when the friendship seems a little worn around the edges. But occasionally several in your group of friends will have to show up at her workplace and do what we call a "purse intervention" and force her to get a new one just to save your group the embarrassment. And if you ever find yourself in Mexico on that spontaneous girl getaway, she will be the one to make sure you don't get left there.

PURSE SCHIZOPHRENIC

This chick changes her purse more often than most people change underwear. Her purses will sometimes have things that light up or make noises. And she likes for her purse to accurately reflect how she feels that day. Often she'll carry a purse inside a purse, just in case her mood changes midday. She never has anything she needs because she left it in her other purse when she was changing them out. She's not the most dependable one in your group of friends but she is the most fun—she's a party waiting for a place to happen, baby! Of course, when you actually *have* a party, she'll never be on time, because she left the invitation in her other purse, "so could you text the address to me?" But when she does finally arrive—the party can officially start because she always brings the party with her. In her purse. And if you ever find yourself in jail down in Mexico, it's normally because of her.

Let's Stay Together

(Because It's Too Hard to Train Someone New)

*B*efore I get into the topic of marriage, I have a confession:

I've never been a bridesmaid. I don't know exactly what this says about me. Could it mean:

A. I wasn't forming meaningful attachments to other marriageable-age females when I was in the eighteen-to-twenty-nine age range? Or

B. All my friends knew that I wouldn't be able to refrain from laughing uncontrollably during the ceremony and didn't want to risk it? Or

C. I gave off the "I will not buy an ugly dress no matter how much I think of you personally" vibe? Or

D. I was always the pianist or soloist.

I think it was probably D. It's easier to find friends that will buy the ugly dress than one who kept up with the piano lessons; since I could play something more elaborate than "Heart and Soul" or "Chopsticks," I was always the wedding musician and never once the bridesmaid. I have considered working up to a full-blown state of feeling that I might have missed out on a wonderful slice of life, but when I take the time to enumerate the duties of the bridesmaid versus the duties of the pianist, I find it hard to complain.

BRIDESMAID	PIANIST
Buy the (usually) ugly dress and all necessary accessories	Provide lovely accompaniment for most important day of bride's life, sometimes even get paid for it!
Attend several showers; purchasing gifts for each shower to show support for your friend, the bride	
Sit through four-hour rehearsal during which you learn where to stand and how fast to process and whose arm you take to recess	
Get hair done to match hair of other bridesmaids, because the bride is looking for total fashion uniformity	
Arrive at wedding early for makeup and photos in 100-degree weather	
Stand for the hour-long ceremony in shoes that really hurt (and which	

are custom-dyed to match the dress;
so you have to wear them to
this wedding, or never!)

Stand for hours at the reception;
by now the feet have swollen and
the straps of the shoes are cutting
off various toes

Remember to take the dress to a
Goodwill store in another town on
Monday

Conclusion—pianist trumps bridesmaid.

I had two bridesmaids in my wedding, and as much as I loved my friends, their big contribution (besides wearing bad lavender dresses that made me seem outstanding by contrast: the true calling of the bridesmaid) was going out to purchase not one but *two* Hershey's chocolate bars to fend off the sudden onset of heretofore unheard-of levels of stress. (In the FYI department, a chocolate bar should be standard issue with the sewing kit, Scotch tape, oscillating fan, and the single-use emergency Valium pill that comes with the bride's dressing room.)

AS LITTLE GIRLS we get the Complete Dream Package reiterated to us over and over and over again. In the fairy tales, in the movies made out of the fairy tales, in the lunch boxes from the

movies from the fairy tales, the message is the same: A whirl-
wind romance will result in an effortless wedding immediately
followed by "happily ever after." The pinnacle, the peak, the pen-
ultimate: beautiful girl + handsome guy = happily ever after. If
this were true, all the beautiful stars who marry other beautiful
stars should have the formula down.

The phrase "and they lived happily ever after" had to have
been created by the writers of children's stories who: (a) didn't have
any more ideas of how to continue the story, or (b) didn't want to
scare the little children with the truth. What they might have
more accurately written was, "and they lived together, learned
how to tolerate each other's idiosyncrasies, overcame urges to do
physical harm, and built a life history together—complete with
intermittent periods of deep affection, interrupted by insane busy-
ness and wild emotional swings between hope and disappoint-
ment (hoping for the best, forgiving the worst)." Look, even if you
find your "soul mate," you will find that his "soul" will gladly let
you fall into the toilet at 2 A.M. if you don't teach him Proper Seat
Etiquette. I am quite sure I never read *that* in any fairy tale.

There are all sorts of ways to foster a happy union. I read
about a couple who had been married for forty-five years and had
raised a brood of eleven children and were blessed with twenty-
two grandchildren. When asked the secret for staying together
all that time, the wife replied, "Many years ago we made a promise that the first one to pack up and leave had to take all the kids."
I guess that would be considered their "prenup." John and I didn't
have one, basically because we came to the marriage with nothin'.
Ours would have had to read, "Should this union dissolve, I'll

take my debts, you take yours." Don't laugh. Some days it was the only thought that kept us hanging on.

There is not much we argue about anymore. In the beginning of our marriage, we used to go at it. Not because we didn't love each other. It was mainly because we are both firstborns. Two firstborns is a tough draw. Neither of us was good at giving ground or conceding which hills were worth dying on. Okay, maybe it was just me who was bad at it, now that I think about it. I needed agreement before I could let a thing go. Such is the folly of youth. I believed that if you were *really* in love and *really* soul mates, there would be this cosmic resonance, filled with huge chunks of *agreement*. What a crock! If only I'd known then that there are about three or four issues that are vital to life and about seven billion other details that don't really matter at all, I could have saved myself (and John!) boatloads of stress. And if I hadn't taken everything so personally those first fifteen years we were married, I feel certain that we would have had a lot more sex. I am trying to make up for it now.

It isn't that we no longer care about ideas or opinions, it's just that—at this point in our marriage—we've already had pretty much every argument: I know what he thinks about any given subject. He knows what I think about almost any given subject. This is a big timesaver. Before we launch into any territory we've ever covered before, we try to remember the last time we discussed it. If no new experiences have occurred that would significantly alter either of our opinions, what is the use of going there again? We find it challenging to try to find new things to argue about.

But there *is* one area that I just can't let go. It's been a source of continual contention.

For the last twenty-seven-plus years, we have been going places in the car together. For the first, oh, say, ten years of our marriage, I think I spent the majority of the time facing toward the back of the car. This was because there was always some sort of child back there in need of a pacifier, juice box, Happy Meal—you know the drill. Small people in backseat = Mom rides facing the back. Now that I am facing *forward* in the car, I have to tell you that it is frightening what is going on up there.

My husband has absolutely no clue that the laws of motion and physics have any bearing on his driving. He somehow believes that all cars will magically move out of his way from the mere force of his will and that we are surrounded by a powerful force field that will make other drivers able to read his mind, project his next driving move, and get the heck out of his way. He seems puzzled that there are people who are not skilled drivers on the roads and immerses himself in pseudopsycho evaluations of every driver surrounding him, which keeps him frustrated and entertained for hours.

Meanwhile, let me say, that in all the time that we've been married, I've never thought there was any woman who could vie for John's attention. Mainly because I'm from Texas and I would probably scratch her eyes out. I would do it in a nice, Christian way, but I would definitely do it. But now—now! There is a woman who rides with us all the time, and frankly, I think she's after my man—it's the GPS girl. She, by the way, is safe somewhere up orbiting Earth on her little satellite, so she has no clue what is actually going on in my vehicle, so, of course, she can afford to be über calm and make me look bad when she leaves it to me to fill in the blanks for her.

ANITA SAYS:	GPS GIRL SAYS:
	Prepare to exit on the left.
You do see, hon, that there are about six lanes between us and that exit, right? You might want to think about putting on a blinker so those people know you need to get over. You need to get over a couple more lanes or we are gonna miss the exit. You gotta get over because I can see the exit. You're not gonna make the exit. There's the exit. You're gonna miss the exit. YOU MISSED THE EXIT!	
	Recalculating.

I ask you, Who could compete with Little Miss Techno-Calm? Not that he would ever marry her. Sure, she's great with directions, but she can't play the piano.

When John and I were dating, he knew that he was preparing to be a minister, and guys who are going into full-time ministry work are on the lookout for certain types of girls who might be well suited to that life. I have no idea what might have given John that idea, but he knew I had one desirable minister's wife skill set: I could play the piano. I guess he thought that was enough to offset my much larger set of liabilities (no edit button between brain and mouth was the most egregious). So we entered into the estate of holy matrimony with no money and lots and lots of love.

John used to meet with couples and go through their pre-marital counseling sessions with them. We used to laugh because all of those books said pretty much the same thing: If you want to have a great marriage, all you really need is great communication. Which would be fine if both parties were speaking the same language. But the gap between woman-speak and man-speak is bigger than that between clients and hairdressers. And the way we approach the things we want to discuss is so different. I don't think John has ever "prepared" for an "intense discussion" (aka "argument") with me. In fact I think he has spent most of his waking hours trying to figure out how to avoid those and always seems genuinely surprised that we "need to talk." On the other hand, I prep. I get my game face on. I think of what it is that I need to say to him and three possible responses. Then I think of three things I could say to each of those responses. Within minutes I am already twenty-seven moves into the conversation, and he doesn't even have a clue we need to talk yet.

Also, my husband of all these years is still laboring under some delusion that if he merely stops talking, somehow the argument is over. Not by a long shot, buddy. The argument has simply "changed venues," from out in the open, where he can control his side of the conversation, to inside my head, where I am now talking for BOTH of us. John still has no clue as to why I can be *more* upset thirty minutes after he's stopped talking. He doesn't have a clue what he's been saying all that time inside my head. He would have been better off to stick with the conversation.

And, after all these years, my husband still cannot grasp the concept of something women refer to as "a good cry." These words next to each other in a sentence will cause a man's head to spontaneously combust. In their minds, all crying is bad and MUST BE STOPPED AT ALL COSTS, although they literally have no idea how to accomplish this. Sometimes they make it worse by trying to solve the problem instead of just administering a liberal dose of empathy. But be forewarned, men, that if you give up and walk away, the ensuing crying will no longer be "a good cry" but one that is now officially your fault because you did not care when it was for no official reason.

I am aware that there must be many, many things I do that irritate my husband, but since he's not writing this book, I get to list mine. Most of mine have to do with irritating words. There are just words that make me grit my teeth and think bad, bad thoughts:

Irregardless.

This is not actually a word. But people think it is. I believe this nonword is a merging of the real word *regardless* (which, by the way, actually means what people are trying to say when they unnecessarily alter it) with the prefix *ir-*, which means "not." So they have, in effect, created a double negative "not not regarding"— which actually means that they ARE regarding it. Which is bass ackwards. Which makes them not irignorant.

Interesting.

John is a full-time abuser of this word. A word that is basically a nonopinion. If I ask his opinion on something, nine times out of ten, John's entire opinion will be "interesting," which I now interpret as either a stall while he is formulating an opinion or while he is trying to figure out a diplomatic way to deliver his true opinion. To John, *interesting* is applicable in almost every situation unless that situation is *boring*—in which case, it could be *interesting*, except that it is wholly devoid of interest.

Whatnot.

Is there any other word that reeks of sheer unmanliness more than *whatnot*? John is totally manly (if you don't count his left-handedness, his love of decorating, and the fact that he will occasionally exfoliate), yet John will throw this word in as an acceptable substitution for *et cetera*. Seriously, can you imagine a general in the army barking at his troops, "Okay, boys, we're gonna take that left ridge with a battery of grenades and missile launchers and whatnot"? Or a quarterback, in a huddle on third down, yelling, "Listen up, guys. We're gonna do the thirty-six-sweep left and then I want you to ram it down their throats, and whatnot!"? I didn't think so.

But, *irregardless* of his *interesting* use of goofy words and *whatnot*, he's the best thing on two legs, and I'm gonna keep him.

Send in the Hissy-Cam

*I*n the theater world, shows that teams of people have poured their hearts and money into for years open and fold in a minute. The elusive Long Run on Broadway is a rarity, indeed. Shows that connect with an audience in such a way that people keep on coming year after year after year are a statistical anomaly. But there are some shows that just don't go away like . . .

The Phantom of the Opera (my husband's personal favorite, although for the life of me I have no idea why). We saw it at the Kennedy Center in Washington, D.C., years ago, and John has been a big fan ever since. I think it might be the rock-and-roll power chords played on a pipe organ—analyze that!

Cats (Never seen it, but I hear it's the pick of the litter. Ba da bing! Rim shot, please!).

Les Misérables (apparently about airplane passengers trapped on a commuter flight with six teething babies).

160

But there is a longer running show than any of these—it's the Mama Drama. This is based on life, since we mamas can ratchet up the drama to the brink of annihilation and are not afraid to initiate a full-scale meltdown every now and then, should the situation warrant it. Mamas can crank up the drama to produce their desired results. We are not afraid to flail about, roll eyes, slam doors, and huff around. Mamas know how to hammer on a point, then drive it home with the perfect just-over-the-top amount of histrionics. It's hard to put the brakes on this production, the Mama Drama, when we have been in it far longer than anyone has been in *Phantom* or *Cats* (though fits of passion and claws do tend to come out in all theater blockbusters).

Coming from the South, I can tell you that southern women excel in their flair for Tony Award–Worthy Mama Drama performances. If you watch any depiction of southern life and there are mothers in the script, there will be sparks and conflicts and storming off and apologies and crying jags and sinking spells and hissy fits. Southern women are not given to emotional temperance. We believe that kind of thing is best left to steady midwesterners, reserved northerners, or laid-back West Coasters. There are women of those regions who can hold their own in the drama department, but as a rule they only occasionally participate in the type of behaviors at which southern women perpetually excel. Think *Steel Magnolias* and *Divine Secrets of the Ya-Ya Sisterhood*.

If we need to hit the pause button in a conflict, we simply develop a sudden case of "the vapors." No one can actually give a medical definition of "the vapors," but we know that it causes us to swoon, temporarily lose focus, and causes someone to get us a glass of iced water (better yet, sweet tea), and it gives us time to collect our thoughts and garner sympathy before we proceed. "The vapors" is uncontestable, as no one knows exactly what it is.

A full-on "hissy fit" is a state that a woman throws herself into completely. It doesn't matter what the precipitating conflict might be, when a woman goes into Hissy Mode, you might as well give up any thoughts of reasoning with her. In a hissy fit, we give full sway to the feeling, and no amount of logic may be applied whatsoever. And note that we always *throw* a hissy fit. It is something hurled from us. When you are "throwing" one, you are definitely putting *everything* you are feeling out there for all the world to see. Men hate to see a woman who is throwing one, but other women find it somewhat amusing to watch.

It's a female spectator sport, and women won't ordinarily intervene, because it's fascinating to see how long one can be sustained. A hissy fit is akin to bull riding at the rodeo: You know it can't last long, but the rider gets more points the longer he's in the saddle. It's the one "sport" women would be tempted to bet on, for duration, but we wouldn't even have time to dig the money out of our wallets. Hissy fits don't normally last long, because it takes an enormous amount of energy to keep that momentum going.

A "sinking spell" is different from "the vapors," as you may actually go limp and lose vision for a couple of seconds during a "sinking spell." It is less than a "faint" but more than a "vapor." My grandmother used to have sinking spells at strategic times (like if she was finding out that someone was pregnant for the fifth time or had just got a tattoo, or both). I always imagined that her sinking spells were low blood sugar in an emotional wrapper, but as I get older, I know that certain pieces of information really can make you go all weak, to where you just need to sit down for a minute.

Each of these distinct conditions can be made less difficult by giving the woman space, rapid fanning, and something called "nerve pills," which can be anything ranging from Skittles to Valium, depending on the victim and the perpetrator.

I offer you this very detailed definition about the various Mama Drama performances only because, should you find yourself in a situation where you need to use one of these dramatic devices, I know you'll want to employ the most appropriate response.

Mamas tend to cross over from the Discussion Mode to the Drama Mode when we perceive that our point of view is either wrong (and we're not going to change it, seeing as how we have become so emotionally invested in defending our position) or that our perspective is not finding an open mind on the other side of the conversation (and we now must make our point more pointedly). When the drama gets to this stage, a mama is not above making mention of intense, long labor, the dangers of childbirth, and permanent stretch marks—or her personal Unforgivables List.

Every woman keeps this list tucked away in the back of her mind, whether she wants to admit it or not. It is a little running tab of some bad things that impacted her greatly at the time they happened.

On my daughter's list there would be at least two entries: I was out of town ON THE DAY of her sixteenth birthday (never mind that we celebrated it for a whole month, I was gone on THE DAY). Also, I sorta kinda ruined the autograph of her favorite hockey player. I mean, who knew that the clear fingernail polish I was putting on the signature he scrawled on her cell phone *in order to preserve it for all time* was actually the only chemical known to mankind that dissolves Sharpie marker? (Andy Sutton, if you ever hear of this, help a mama get one unforgivable off the list.) And I have a little list going with Elyse, as I have *not* forgotten the day (I think she was about nine years old) when she came into the bathroom, took one look at my pj'd body, and stated, "Wow, Mom. I totally get why you wear a bra."

Holidays and Holi-Don'ts

There's an old Elvis Presley Christmas song (well, Elvis sang it; Red West wrote it) that goes like this: "Oh why can't every day be like Christmas?" It's a beautiful song, but the answer to the question seems obvious. Why can't every day be like Christmas? I'll tell you why. *Because we couldn't bear it.* If every day *were* like Christmas, we would be bleary-eyed from late-night toy assemblies, neurotic and overwrought from biting our tongues around visiting relatives, jittery about the impending credit card statements, bloated from the sweets at the requisite parties, and worried about our children's ability to survive their prosperity.

Christmas is supposed to be "the most wonderful time of the year," and in many ways, it is. There is a certain pervasive goodwill that is extended to friends and strangers alike.

Unless, that is, they are vying for the last parking spot near the front of the mall.

There is but one category of people who do not participate in the Last Space in the Parking Lot Quest—

because all their shopping is already done, don'tcha know? Let's give a shout-out and props to that group: the Organized Christmas People (aka The OCPs). These are people whose obsessive-compulsive tendencies become an advantage rather than a disorder at Christmastime; at Christmas, the rest of us would aspire to even half of their organizational skills. OCPs have Christmas savings accounts, with automatic monthly deposits deducted painlessly from their bimonthly paychecks, so they awaken on October 1 to find their Christmas fund is loaded and ready to fire. The highest order of OCPs, though, *don't even need that Christmas account money*; their shopping is fully completed during the Labor Day Weekend Sales and their gifts wrapped and stacked before October 1. For them, the Christmas account money is pure bonus savings.

These people cannot be my friends. Mainly because they cannot stop talking about how relaxed their holidays are. If they had any people skills, they would learn to keep it to themselves.

OCPs use lists (and by this I mean "fat accounting ledgers"— aka the Yule Log) filed according to year. The Yule Log includes: who they sent Christmas cards to, what they have purchased for people in years past, sizes and color preferences, each person's reaction to each present, files for receipts, and potential gift ideas for upcoming years. The Christmas season is a chance for an OCP to show off her high-achiever ranking. It is an Organized Christmas Person's World Championship, so to speak.

I have a friend who is like this. I had to ask Stacy to explain her list of Yule Log categories to me, since otherwise I would have no idea where to begin to make such lists. For people like Stacy, that ledger is just a normal part of the holiday season—

same as looking high and low for receipts is a normal part of my season. For people like me who fit neatly into the category of nonplanner (aka FBSPs—Fly By the Seat of Pants people), Christmas is an ever so slightly more muddled experience.

Organizational experts seem to agree that the best way to bring order to the chaos that can accompany the holidays is summed up in a single word: *simplify*. They close their eyes when they say it, as if to convey the utter Zen-like peace that will sweep over your life if you *just* pare things down to the essentials. (Have you ever noticed, however, that the people urging you to "simplify" are also the ones who want you to buy their complex product lines of books and videos and planners?)

Still, our family thought these simplifiers might be on to something, so we started our own crusade to do less. Our first decision was to ditch the whole Christmas card thing. Our rationale was that anyone who is truly close to us will be receiving a Christmas present from us in the mail, or we'll be seeing them over the holidays; thus, no "greeting" card necessary. This leaves a great number of people in the "We Haven't Contacted You All Year Because There's Really No Reason To" category. We figured that these people probably wouldn't want a Christmas card from us, as it would only serve to remind them that we didn't like them enough to keep in touch, thus reopening the social wound. We thought, *Why make it worse?* So we have the two categories— Those Who Don't Need a Card Because They Know That We Love Them versus Those Who Probably Don't Need a Card to Remind Them How We Haven't Cared Enough to Contact Them All Year Long. Simple enough, right? Thus we dispensed with the Christmas cards.

This, however, does not stop us from *receiving* Christmas cards. And we love that, because we know we must fall into one of those categories with all the people who send them to us! It's our own little family game, trying to decide which we are.

I have started trying to respond with a personal letter in January to all the people who personally *signed* their cards, instead of having their signatures printed. I think that people who have their signatures printed are the laziest of the lazy. (Yes, if you can believe this—somehow even lazier than those of us who don't send any Christmas cards at all!) It's okay if the card is from your dentist's office, but it's highly impersonal if the sender is Joe Q. Friend. Yes, my family and I are holiday card snobs, but one has to uphold some standards in one's life. We also give bonus points to anyone who includes a family picture with their card. There is lots of cheer to be gotten from watching the hairlines and waistlines creep one way and the other from year to year.

We also receive quite a few of those Christmas newsletters. Oh, joy. We have a few friends who make theirs into a poem, with a rhyme scheme. I don't think I could make my year's events rhyme—like, what rhymes with *catheter*? We have other friends who make their newsletters a pictorial year in review. They Photoshop themselves into an enviable variety of exotic climes (can anyone really vacation that much?). The mail I wait for every Christmas is from a woman who writes a *very long* newsletter, in the third person (as if we didn't know that she is writing it), about how amazing and brilliant and beautiful her children are (they might be) and how fabulous their family life is (it might be) and how spiritual her life is (*hours* of Bible study daily), blah, blah, blah. I'm sure you get these, too.

Reality TV shows are so popular; why can't we have reality Christmas newsletters? Just once I'd like to receive a letter that says, "We've had a mixed bag this year—lots of life lessons, some ups and downs with our kids, and a few setbacks financially. My husband's hair transplant wasn't the success we were hoping for, but it looks pretty good over the top of one ear. So how are you?"

And the question we simply must address today is this: At what age is it appropriate for children to balk at the insistence of their parents making them take a picture with the mall-variety Santa Claus?

Exhibit A: A friend of mine receives a Christmas card every year from a fine, upstanding family here in Georgia. When she first began receiving their family Christmas photo (more than two decades ago), the boys were small and the photos of them with Santa were fun. Now, these boys are well into their thirties, with wives and young families of their own. One is in medical school, the other is an executive with a bright future; but they still pose every year (at their mother's insistence) for their brotherly photo with Santa.

What say you? Cute, or just plain sick?

ANOTHER EFFORT to simplify our family's holidays has actually made them more complicated. A few years back, we had a semibrilliant idea—to find one really great gift, buy it in multiples, and give it to just about everyone on our list. As I said, it seemed like a brilliant idea, but sometimes we have a few left over; we save them in bins in the attic. The problem is, when Christmas comes 'round again, we can't remember if people were on the list last year, or if they've become better friends in the interim and thus should receive this year the great thing from last year. It's maddening. So, if we meet you somewhere this year, remind us at Christmastime that you are a "newer friend" because we've got a lot of great gifts in the attic just waiting for a whole new batch of lucky recipients.

Far, far away from these troubles of an FBSP, there lives a particular breed of OCPs who are the ultracool, the ultimately confident: They order their gifts via the World Wide Web and ship everything straight to the door of each loved one, perfectly packed and impeccably wrapped. They do not break a sweat, neither emotionally nor physically, while questing for an appropriate gift. They put on pajamas, brew a cup of chai, and click their way to Christmas Gift Easy Street. If they are out among the riffraff on Christmas Eve, it is merely to take in the sights and sounds and thank the Lord that they are not like the rest of us. (Christmas Pharisees.) If you are one of these people, please try to curb your feelings of superiority.

The rest of us view the Christmas shopping experience as a decathlon. And even this challenge might not be so bad if the Parking Lot Stalk-a-Spot Race were not on the docket. But it is.

Parking lots at Christmastime are not the place to view peace on earth or peace of mind. They are more like piece-of-my-mind. At this time of year, the mere sight of a mall parking lot brings out the predator in everyone. The parking situation is a classic study in supply and demand. There are a limited number of spaces and more-than-the-usual number of would-be occupants. So how do we find a spot? We stalk the people walking out to their cars. (Don't act like you don't do it. You know you do.) We see them crossing in front of the store headed for their car and we turn up the row with them and go *v-e-r-y s-l-o-w-l-y* so as not to tip them off that we are stalking them. If they turn around to look at us, we look the other way. This stealth operation goes on until they either cut across to another row (how dare they?) or arrive at their car, only to open the trunk, deposit some bags from the Toting Event, and wave us off as they mouth the words, "I'm not leaving."

Coises. Foiled again. We are doomed to continue circling the lot, like buzzards, for another thirty minutes, waiting for the next stalkable person to appear. I believe that all the Faux Leave-ers should identify themselves as such before they get to their cars. Can't we get some legislation to require that?

Once a space does open up (for a nanosecond), it becomes a struggle for supremacy between The Quicker (any car with a small turn radius and thin body) versus The Bigger (SUVs and all other vehicles with names that evoke testosterone). The smaller cars have the advantage in the agility department, but the large bodies can intimidate merely by the fact that they can squish a Prius like a soda can.

Much as I admire the OCPs, my FBSP ways may be too entrenched to be rehabilitated. If I find a preprinted Yule Log with an interactive chip that automatically registers every purchase, files every receipt, and logs each recipient response, I *might* see my way clear to better holiday organization and an earlier finish to the shopping list.

'Til then, when Christmastime comes, I'll be stalking you.

So I Married Santa Claus

A lot of subliminal factors go into choosing a life partner. Some scientists tell us that women choose a husband based on facial proportions and symmetrical features. Other researchers contend that we choose based on particular scents, scents that are difficult to identify but are strongly tied to our childhoods. Some women choose a man based on how much he reminds her of her father. I think I married John because he was as close as I could get to Santa Claus.

I'm not saying that he's fat and jolly. Quite the opposite. He is a lean, not-at-all-mean lovemaking machine. What I mean is that he loves Christmas with childlike abandon and isn't ashamed to exhibit that love. And though his vocational choice was to be in church ministry and then become my road manager, he definitely has a second calling in Display/Décor. He's a little bit "metro," but in the best possible way.

He has created his own niche within the "metrosexual" definition. He was raised in Mississippi and cannot deny his Rankin County roots, but he can decorate circles around my female friends. I call him my little "Redneck Metrosexual." For example, he loves to change the monthly display on the front hall table to match the seasons *and* he has no problem shooting squirrels off our back deck. We are the only people I know who have a pump-action BB gun behind the drapes next to the French doors so John can run out and shoot, Jed Clampett–style. He has yet to do this in his underwear, but I'm sure it's just a matter of time. I would like to take this time to apologize to each of our neighbors who have witnessed John's Pavlovian response to the lowly squirrel. He does loathe them so.

But having a Redneck Metrosexual Man makes me envied among neighborhood women. Last Halloween I was at the door, greeting the little trick-or-treaters from our cul-de-sac. As some newer neighbors followed their little cutie pies to our door, one of the women commented that they all love the way we leave our front door open so they can view the table that changes every month and enjoy the beautiful decorations that signal the up-coming season. She said, "I know you guys travel a lot and I just don't know how you do it!" I just shook my head and said, "I *don't*, but I'll be happy to call my husband up here so you can tell him how much you like it." I wish I had a Polaroid of her face. It was as if I had just told her that my husband *was* Martha Stewart. I'm sure he'll be invited to give a demonstration at the women's club any day now.

So when Christmas rolls around, John sees it as the Olympics of Decorating. Not as in, "I will put up more lights and yard ornaments than anyone on my block," but more like, "My house will be the most elegantly decorated in my neighborhood." As we spent seven years of our married life in Virginia, he devotes a great deal of time to putting together a Williamsburg-esque half-round of fruit that goes over our front door. It has magnolia leaves, oranges, lemons, apples, pears, and a pineapple in the middle (which is great if the weather stays cold; if it warms up, fruit sap drips on our heads whenever we leave the house). I am always tempted to eat the fruit John picks out for this project, which is probably why he doesn't let me help with it anymore. He also makes fresh pine swags that surround the front door and trains spotlights on it so that it is accentuated just so. He nestles spotlighted carolers near the walkway, hangs matching wreaths from every outside window, and puts Williamsburg lights on each windowsill. This consumes an entire Saturday, and that's before he starts inside the house.

When his attention turns indoors, no surface (flat or otherwise) is safe. He decorates everything. There is Christmas paraphernalia everywhere you look. It's a wonderful thing.

John's Christmas enthusiasm extends to his ability to make the season last from Thanksgiving Saturday 'til Valentine's Day. He has, on certain years, presented each of us with Twelve Days of Christmas presents (not the actual calling birds and French hens, but a present for each of the days leading up to Christmas Day). I remember one of his friends asking John to consider backing off on the pre-Christmas gift giving because the friend's wife was asking why *he* didn't give *her* a dozen gifts!

Our penchant as southerners to leave the Christmas lights up on our houses all year long is so clichéd that our fellow Georgians actually use it as a redneck measure. If you don't leave your lights up, you're not in the club. I understand the leave-'em-up rationale though. Once you've risked life and limb to string those lights, it seems smart to just leave them up. Besides, the older I get, the closer together Christmases seem to be; it feels like we just got the decorations put up before it's time to get them back down again. Some people describe it à la the Quantum Toilet Paper Roll Theorem: The less paper is left on the roll, the faster it goes.

But it's not the lights attached to the rooftops in February that really make you a redneck; it's the plastic Santa, Frosty, and Rudolph on the front lawn that you have to mow around in July.

I am thankful to have a man who truly enjoys all that the season brings and who has given our kids such a strong launching pad for their own traditions. I have a button that reads I STRIVE TO LIVE EVERY DAY AS IF IT WERE MY BIRTHDAY. John strives to live every day as if it were Christmas.

Orna-mental

Ah, the quest for the Perfect Christmas Tree. For some, it involves a trip to the local Christmas tree farm to see them growing live, judge them like they're modeling for a Miss Christmas Tree pageant, take a hand saw to the base of the favored tree, cut it down in the prime of its life, and bring it home caveman style. For others, the quest involves visiting the local roadside stands (trees that have been carted in from the nether regions) and choosing from a lovely selection of various pines and evergreens. At this point you must decide if you will choose to support the local Boy Scout troop and pay twenty dollars extra, or go down to the Home Depot and live with your Scrooge-ishness.

There are many who choose to forgo the yearly tree choice trauma. They have gone artificial and never have to wrestle with the tree stand, deal with dropping needles, or remember to water. They also have the option of storing their tree with its lights on from year to year, though this can backfire when the lights become tangled around the tree. We have actually resorted to scissors to get those tightly wound light strings off an artificial tree. This may seem overly dramatic, but getting them off any other way takes too much time.

Do you recall when strings of lights cost a lot of money? About ten years ago they went from a $12-a-box proposition down to $2.99 per box. I believe that was the exact time we decided that it was *not* worth it to sit around on the floor for an hour with a bulb tester, trying to find the one bulb that was out.

Trying to pin down the genesis of tree decorating is a little slippery, but most scholars point to Germany as the country of origin. The evergreen coming indoors was (at first) a pagan ritual to bring the only green thing in the dead of winter indoors to celebrate life. Christians appropriated that ritual around the time of Martin Luther—he added lights and some other decorations. (What a feather in his cap—illuminating the concept of grace *and* decorating the Christmas tree.)

When we were newlyweds, John and I lived in housing for married college students. These duplexes might as well have had a sign hanging outside that read, IF YOU ARE HARE-BRAINED ENOUGH TO BELIEVE THAT YOU CAN HOLD DOWN THREE PART-TIME JOBS, CRAM FOR EXAMS, *and* NURTURE A MARRIAGE, THE LEAST WE CAN DO IS GIVE YOU LOW-COST SHELTER WITH GAS HEAT, WHICH MAY OR MAY NOT ASPHYXIATE YOU. We worked on our little duplex for a few weeks before we got married (between semesters) and made our little love nest as cozy as a forty-year-old-half-a-house could be. I recently drove down that street and saw that the college had bulldozed our duplexes and sold the property for frontage for a superstore. And we worked so hard on that vinyl floor . . .

Our very first Christmas tree was a true Charlie Brown Special. I don't mean *the Charlie Brown Christmas Special* (the one on TV with the great Vince Guaraldi Skating Song and the children singing "Christmas time is here . . ."). I mean the Charlie Brown Christmas *tree*. The last one left on the lot, with very little left in the pine needle department. Our little tree smelled great; there were about eighteen inches between each of its branches. That sounds sad, but it worked well. We had practically nothing but a string of lights and a few "Our First Christmas Together 1982" ornaments to hang on it. We had no idea that we were being historically accurate, but this sort of tree was *preferred* in the 1600s in Germany because the only lights they had on their trees were candles, and who wants to have an indoor bonfire for Christmas?

With the birth of each of our children came the accompanying ornaments celebrating each baby's entrance into the world, then came all the ornaments they crafted for us with their widdle hands. Some were cute, some were . . . they were definitely original. We hung the cute ones in conspicuous places on the tree. The less cute ones had their own place of honor—it's called the Backside of the Tree. We used to tell the kids that we put these ornaments on the window side for everyone to see as they passed by the house. Cruel, I know.

Hallmark stores came up with a great marketing tool: offering numerous ornaments with the year inscribed on them. We bought these for half price after the holidays because we liked the way they looked, never projecting that this would be a problem. We have one with BABY'S FIRST CHRISTMAS 1987—the hitch being that we didn't *have* a baby that year. Our kids became confused. They thought we were hiding other siblings from them. I'll have to get a Sharpie and fix those ornaments someday.

Handmade ornaments are coveted items in some circles. I have friends who go to parties where the only entertainment is that everyone exchanges ornaments they have made themselves. This is risky unless you are selective in your guest list.

Even if you are the Queen of Crafts and have a magazine and television show celebrating your craft prowess, you can have an off day. I read on a Web news page that the formerly incarcerated domestic diva Martha Stewart participated in the Christmas decorating contest at her prison. She and her fellow elves didn't have an actual tree to decorate (prison rules don't permit them, as I suppose they could be fashioned into battering rams), but they didn't want to miss out on being orna-mental even behind bars. Each group of prisoners was given twenty-five dollars' worth of glitter, ribbons, construction paper, and glue. Martha instructed her cellmates to make origami cranes. ("Jody—no, no, no. You fold the upper corner down toward your leg irons and fold the right corner toward your tattoo.") They hung the cranes across the ceiling and in front of the (barred) window. What could Martha Stewart have been thinking—as if the judges wouldn't infer a reference to "jailbirds"? Martha's group suffered an embarrassing defeat. Awww. That must have been a little hard to swallow for Ms. It's-a-Good-Thing.

I HAVE SEEN (only in movies) that there are some people who don't put their trees up until Christmas Eve. Who *are* these people? Don't they know that part of the joy of having a tree is its being up at least a couple of weeks prior to Christmas so you can enjoy the lights and watch the presents and pine needles stack up around the bottom? And these late tree-putter-uppers are the same people who take the tree down the day after Christmas. They obviously don't decorate as much as we do, because if we waited until Christmas to do all that we do, then took the tree down immediately afterward, we would miss Christmas altogether. I believe that these people are secretly Christmas haters. They want to have the least amount of Christmas environment allowable by law. Their mantra is: "It's not Christmas yet, not yet, not yet, not yet—now it is—great, it's over already—get the stuff outta here!" We leave our tree lights on twenty-four hours a day, and we don't care if our electricity bill spikes for several weeks. Some things are just worth it.

Our family has now reached the stage in tree-trimming evolution where a single tree will not accommodate the ornaments we have made, collected, been given, or bought at the after-Christmas sales. We now have the following trees in different rooms of our house:

- *The Family Tree* in the living room—a real, live tree with ornaments of sentimental value.
- *The Gingerbread Tree* in the kitchen—small and spindly, artificial, with food-related ornaments such as dried orange slices—and I swear this is true—dried okra pods with Santa faces painted on them.
- *The Music/Victorian/White House Official Yearly Ornament Tree* in the dining room—artificial pencil tree that fits neatly in any corner or window without taking up

extra space. We decorate this tree with uppity ornaments that do not disturb our digestion.

- *The Snowman-Stuff-Got-to-Be-Too-Much-for-the-Entryway-Table Tree* in the front hall—another artificial tree purely for passersby to enjoy.

Our multiple-tree scenario might not seem reminiscent of our early uncomplicated Christmases, but all these trees represent our desire to celebrate in every room of our home. If we could just get the laundry room theme going, we would have it all covered. Besides, you can't let the different species of ornaments commingle or intermarry. They will be confused.

Ho, Ho, Home Improvements

When I went to Graceland a couple of years ago, I learned many interesting facts about Elvis (he loved karate, wanted to be an undercover narcotics agent, he had a chimpanzee—these things are unrelated). One that stands out in my memory is that Elvis never allowed anyone except his close friends and family members to go upstairs in his home. If you wanted to see Elvis, you had to wait downstairs. Having had a few holiday open houses myself, I see the wisdom of the Elvis Rule.

Open houses are a good idea taken to an illogical extreme. It is, indeed, a good thing to hospitably welcome people to enter your home. It is not, however, a good idea to give a group of people a free pass to look in all your closets and poke around your home like it's a museum. If we only had velvet ropes to establish boundaries.

When we were on church staff, we always opened our home to the entire congregation one night around the holidays. We would prepare all sorts of food, and we would clean the house until we were in a tizzy. All this so we could stand for hours welcoming people while also trying to keep from passing out from the cleaning-induced fatigue. At least the open house was a great excuse to get our house spic-and-span (well, my version, at least), to decorate, and to complete projects that had been on the running to-do list all year.

But I seem to have a very special holiday-related affliction similar to SAD (Seasonal Affective Disorder, which causes people to become depressed when they don't receive enough sunlight). I get something called RAD (Remodeling Affective Disorder). This is a mental disorder that propels type-A people to do in the last quarter of the year all the household projects that they have been meaning to do all year, spurred on by the guarantee of having company over the holidays. A built-in deadline is imposed when we expect open-housers and relatives to arrive.

If there were drugs to stop this insanity, my husband would have bought stock in the company. He, unfortunately, is the one who gets stuck executing my "unique and artistic" ideas (read: "no instructions available") while he desperately needs—and wants—to finish his own decorating for the holidays. You can cut the conflict with a putty knife.

In our almost three decades of marriage, we have come to accept many of our differences and actually learned to appreciate several of them, but in our approaches to problem solving we have distinctly opposite preferences about how you reach resolution. The need to tackle household projects during the holidays may be one arena in our marriage where John has decided to just go with the strangeness; this eventually works to the good of the household (if he can survive it). Besides, any excuse to spend time at Home Depot beats no excuse. Hardware stores are the nondrinker's bar. All the guys there know your name. And they're really glad you came. It's good for John's ego, too. He tells me that every time he goes down the laser stud-finder aisle, the lasers all point to him as he walks by.

A couple of years ago the home-improvement plan got a little more involved than either of us had envisioned, but John proved heroic. When my friends talk about being "into rocks," they are talking about diamonds. But when I talk about being "into rocks," I am referring to big stones that you can dig up out of the ground. Lately, I have been requesting that John create all sorts of things out of rocks. (I think rocks make me feel more connected to the area of central Texas where I grew up.) John made me a rock waterfall and patio in the backyard. Then I thought we needed to move the rock creativity indoors. All the way into our bedroom.

I don't know where I came up with this idea, but I wanted to take out the carpet in our bedroom and have John lay a random tile floor. This made perfect sense in my mind's eye. Tiles of varying shades and sizes would make the floor look unique and artisan-ish. When we went to the tile store to quest for said tiles, there was a dreadful math word problem awaiting me. Remember when we were in fifth grade and we got hit with the sort of word problem that read, "If John is going to lay a random tile floor for his nutsy wife and the room is 14 feet by 24 feet, will he need tile sizes that are divisible by 3 inches or by 4 inches?" This math problem was my idea of a living hell. (Math was a nightmarish component I had not foreseen in my "random" and "artisan" visions.) Fortunately there were many mathly males standing around, with calculators at the ready, perfectly willing to attempt feats of math magic. After much scratching of heads, we decided to go with the tiles that were multiples of 3.

My man trucked the tiles home and started the weeklong process of removing the old carpet, laying the subfloor for two whole days—also, not in my vision—and then we started the portion of the work that would bring this glorious Tuscan floor to fruition: the laying of the tile. It was hard. Really hard. My commitment to randomness meant that I had chosen tiles of different thicknesses, so John had to carefully level every one to match the one next to it. This process took two days, and much staring to make sure that no two similar pieces were side by side.

By the time the floor was finished and grouted, John had literally worked his buns off. I am not exaggerating. They're gone and may never make a comeback. And, as we have aged, we've developed a scale that represents how many anti-inflammatory agents we have to ingest to bring a project to completion. We call it "the Celebrex Factor." This floor scored off that chart. But my beautiful Italian tile floor looks *bellissimo,* and it is one of a kind. When he finished and saw how great it looked, I asked John if he would ever do it for money. He shook his head and replied, "Only for love."

Now if I could just get him to agree to make our bedroom complete with the installation of a perpetual-chocolate fountain. He has agreed in theory, but he made me promise to delay until his Valentine's Affective Disorder kicks in.

And You Made This Yourself?

*I*f you take a roomful of thirty female test subjects and hook them up to pulse monitors with little diodes that measure emotional responses to different words, and one of those words is *handcrafts*, the responses will fall into one of three categories: One-third of the women will be repulsed, one-third will have no measurable response, and one-third will begin openly salivating. This third group, the eager, salivating women, believes that if instructions exist, they can make any project.

I should have known that I was not in this category when I had to ask a friend to reinstall my zipper on the final project for seventh-grade home economics class. (Why does it matter if the zipper zips *up* to the closed position as long as it closes? Zipping down to close is novel. Home ec teachers have no imagination.) But, I confess, my teenage experience did not clue me in to my almost complete lack of craftiness. Consequently, I devoted many holiday seasons of my adulthood to making Christmas gifts. This was, in part, because for the first ten years of our marriage, John and I were inordinately unwealthy. I've heard people wax nostalgic for the happiness they felt when they were young and in love, poor but happy. Not me. I have a Technicolor recollection of the Sonic burgers, Frito chili pies, and Tater Tots. The resulting gastric distress was an element of "young, poor, and in love" that I do not miss. We were this level of poor because we had mucho student loans and babies and because John was a youth pastor. Most churches don't pay youth pastors much money. They pay you in fun. You know what a joy it is to take forty-seven teenagers to camp, right? And lock-ins? (Those all-night youth events where they lock the adults in so they can't escape?) Who doesn't leap at the opportunity to supervise those?

So, back in the day, I would start planning my crafty forays in September. I would quest for types of crafts that I could do successfully. (My options were limited: I cannot paint or sew anything more than a straight line.) I used to (I am not making this up—there are witnesses) drive an hour to the Moormont Apple Orchard, pick apples, take them home, slice them thin with a deli meat slicer, dip them in salt water with lemon juice added (to keep them from turning dark), lay them on drying screens in a warm oven with a wooden spoon wedging the oven door open, leave them there overnight, turn them in the morning to finish fully drying them, then take them out and string them onto garlands in between dried orange slices, drilled whole nutmegs, and dried whole bay leaves. I cannot explain why I did this. I just did.

I also made wondrous cinnamon/applesauce/glue ornaments (rolled out and cut into cookie shapes), hanging dolly heads (made out of cornstarch, baking soda, and water, rolled into balls, baked until hard, faces painted on, straw hair glued on), rosebud topiaries (if you glue 765 dried rosebuds to a Styrofoam ball, you can cover it completely, but *why?*).

The energy these creations required was an amount of energy that I will never experience again. Does such behavior officially qualify as insanity? What made me think this was a great use of my time? It must have been all the *Country Living* magazines I pored over, every one extolling the charms of the country life, replete with beeswax candles, lye soap, and knotty pine furniture. I should have bought different magazines—*Simple Living* or *Lazy Ladies' Journal.*

My craftiest friends would organize a craft show around Thanksgiving time to make money for purchasing Christmas gifts. I was not anal enough to be an organizer, but I participated. Perpetrated. The things left over from the show were a ready-made inventory for fulfilling our own Christmas lists for friends and family.

For all my friends and family who received those handmade items and thought they were lame but were kind enough to display them in prominent areas of their homes when I came to visit, I offer this public apology, and thank you for loving me enough to compromise your décor.

Sometimes we craft-sellers would trade things among our tables in order to have a greater variety of stuff to give to the people on our Christmas lists. That was tricky, since some items were definitely more desirable than others and you had to seem enthused about trading for the lesser desirables. There was one girl who was a great painter, and we *all* wanted her stuff. I think I fell somewhere in the middle of the food chain; my stuff wasn't the best, but it wasn't the worst, either. None of us realized then that if we hadn't spent so much money on raw materials for the crafts, we could have had money to buy Christmas presents for everyone on our lists. You know, gifts they actually wanted.

One scary thing about Christmastime is that it somehow compels even the Far-Less-Than-Crafty to try their hand at the Homemade Gift Category. Was this psychologically ingrained in us when we made all those ornaments as children? How else could we have become such zombies, mindlessly drawn toward the craft store to do things we would not do any other time of the year? Why else would it be that when we see tinsel-draped decorations in store windows and smell pine from trees brought indoors, we feel an uncontrollable desire to reach for scissors, glue, and glitter? And the results are mixed. When your friends have to *ask* you what "it" is, you may have missed.

Some of my friends give culinary gifts. They spend hours in their kitchens preparing home-baked breads accompanied by homemade flavored oils, homemade jellies or gourmet vinegars, which they present in lovely jars with printed labels. These people need therapy. One year it became apparent to me that my crafty gifts weren't getting the same level of response as in years past, so I decided to switch over to gifts of food. Well, maybe I was just hungry. Whatever the reason, food *is* a basic human need. And a gift of food is not as likely to clash with someone's wallpaper as a Styrofoam candy cane studded with multicolor beads.

That first year as a food giver, I scoured recipe books for something novel to bake and found a few recipes for biscotti (for those who do not frequent Starbucks, these are basically doggie biscuits for people). I baked a quantity of biscotti in several flavors, purchased clear corsage boxes, placed a paper doily on the bottom, filled each box with biscotti, and tied the whole thing up with some lovely fabric ribbon. I was sure that I had hit upon the perfect food gift. These dehydrated Italian sweet biscuits are in all the coffee shops these days, but around 1993 I found myself having to explain to the confused recipients exactly what they were.

"They're Italian. They're *supposed* to be dried out. Yes, on purpose."

I might have been slightly ahead of my time, but the truth is probably that most of my friends and family didn't really want a variety pack of human doggie biscuits to have with their coffee, no matter the year, no matter how cute the packaging.

My last experiment in homemade gifts involved sugar bath products. After strolling through Bath and Body Works and reading the ingredient list on one of their eighteen-dollar sugar scrubs, I felt certain that I could replicate their formula for a lot less money. This is precisely the sort of thinking that always gets me in trouble.

So I trekked to the health food store (aka Most Expensive Place to Purchase Anything) and bought raw sugar (turbinado), almond and avocado oils, and assorted other essential oils for scenting. I also spent money on containers with strong seals (you wouldn't want the oil leaking onto the shower floor, thereby creating a post-holiday disaster when no one has met their deductible in January). I was set. The mixing of the sugar scrubs was a wonderful experience (my hands were never so soft—an added bonus), and the packaging was no problem, either. I will just leave you with the lesson that I learned from this homemade gift: No matter how tight that seal seems to be, ants like sugar scrub, too.

My friends, it is up to you to decide if you are a true crafty or just a wannabe. Look for the telltale signs in your recipients' responses and comments:

- Do they smile wanly as they turn the item a full 360-degree rotation?
- Do they make general comments such as, "Well, would you look at that?"
- Do they close their eyes while mentally grasping for adjectives to describe it?
- Do they accidentally/on purpose "forget" their present when they are leaving?

If so, you may need to come to terms with your less-than-crafty status. Don't think of this as a journey away from the craft store so much as a journey toward your truer nature. If we were all great at handmade gifts, there would be no need for the mall.

To Regift or Not to Regift

(Or, If Only the Wise Men Had Known About Gift Cards)

*L*ast Christmas my mom got a family gift for us: a battery-operated pepper mill. When you press the button on top, it makes a lovely whirring sound and sends a mist of finely ground pepper onto your waiting entrée. It is a little mechanical marvel, but it caused me to wonder: Exactly how lazy *are* we that we can't turn the twist top on a pepper mill to grind our pepper?

While browsing a catalog recently, I saw a ceramic ice-cream-cone holder that had a battery-operated twirler built right in. With this gizmo, you wouldn't even have to turn your wrist to put the perfect lick on your ice cream. Lazy. This is almost as bad as the radio controls built into the steering wheels of new model cars. Have we decided that leaning forward two inches to extend our finger to the position where the radio controls used to be is just too much trouble? Lazy. And how about our latest mascara packaging: oscillating mascara wands? Do we really need a battery-operated wand to jiggle a little when we are putting it on our eyelashes?

And if you are a female applying mascara in the car, isn't the car already doing that for you? Lazy!

Where did these lazy ideas come from?

In every family unit, there are people who are the gift "idea" people and there are those who are the "go out and retrieve the items that the idea person thought up" people. I fall into the "idea" category. I envision a great gift for someone, and then if I can't order it online, I send John out to find it. This was especially handy when the kids were small, since I am allergic to toy stores. As I recall, I had to shop in a Toys "R" Us only once in all the years that my kids were little. Something about the smell of plastic causes me to have a meltdown. I just want to get outta there. Even toy departments in discount stores give me hives. John, conversely, ever the kid at heart, loved to go into Toys "R" Us and test out the toys—you know, "just to be sure that toy is something the kids will like." He is supremely in touch with his inner nine-year-old.

I've also never understood the people who are hung up on the concept of "educational toys." I have friends who quested for weeks to find a toy that would raise their child's IQ a few points. And why is it that anything labeled EDUCATIONAL costs a *lot* more money? Then it languishes at the bottom of the toy chest while the kids happily bang wooden spoons on cookware. My theory about "educational toys" is this: They're for *children*, not graduate students. At the childhood stage of life, *everything* is educational.

Unfortunately, though, a child's attraction to any toy *will* be directly proportional to the number of annoying sounds said toy makes. This results from a conspiracy between the toy manufacturers and the pain reliever companies.

And I define "loss of innocence" as the point in time when children discover the difference between a cheap gift and an expensive one. It's a sad, expensive day. As kids' ages increase, so will the cost of their "toys." Computers and MP3 players and cameras and cell phones are now the items that top their lists. We now deposit gift cards for Best Buy in the kids' stockings so they can indulge their needs for all things electronic.

Personally, I love receiving gift cards, because I consider shopping a sport of sorts. Seriously—think about it. You have a "goal" in mind as you shop—you must beat the other shoppers to the one thing left in your size—and you "score" when you find something you really need on sale. When they start a TV channel that features world-class shopping competitions with corporate sponsors and commentators, I'll TiVo that in a heartbeat.

But the rise of the gift card and the gift certificate on America's Christmas lists is exhibit A regarding confused twenty-first-century messaging. Receiving a gift card *could* mean any of these things:

- "I know that you love to shop and I knew that this would make you happy."
- "I wanted to get you something, but didn't want to go to a *lot* of trouble."
- "I wanted to give you a present, but I don't really know your taste and didn't want to risk getting you something that would result in one of those, 'Oh, how nice,' moments."

- "You're just too difficult to shop for."
- "I *didn't* get you anything, but I had these emergency gift cards stashed away just in case someone like you popped up on the Christmas list."
- "I didn't *want* to get you anything, and this is as close as I could get to nothing."

It's hard to say which meaning a gift card might carry. I suppose it depends on who gives it to you. For the parents of teenagers or young adults, gift cards are an answer to a prayer. We know that our kids will have a great time getting something that we have never heard of, would never approve of, and won't have to return.

Gift cards are also a virtually effortless regifting commodity. To regift anything other than gift cards requires tedious record keeping: You have to write down who the gift is from and whether it has any personalization (how bad would *that* be . . .). You have to be certain that it goes to someone in another geographic region who has absolutely no personal connection to the person who gave it to you. Regifting of anything *other* than a gift card is so tricky that almost no one has done it successfully more than once.

One item that is sure to get regifted, though, is any article of jewelry (other than actual diamonds; you can hardly go wrong with those). You may think you know someone's taste in jewelry, but you probably only know what she *used* to like. Fashions change so quickly that the things we wear now aren't the things we will aspire to wear in the future, and this means that your jewelry recipient is going to have to *pretend* to like a gift of jewelry in your presence, then she'll stick it in her regift pile. She will regift it to someone whose jewelry taste *she* is only guessing at, and *that* recipient will pretend to like it and then add it to *her* regift pile. This pin or necklace or bracelet or earrings might eventually work its way back into the hands of the original purchaser (i.e., you) through the long, winding paths of the regifting process. I suggest making a special mark on the back of the card the jewelry is attached to just so you'll know it's the same one.

Why don't we start a campaign to do away with the social stigma associated with regifting? Is it truly a gift-giving shame, or a brilliant form of recycling? I mean, haven't we all been the recipients of a gift that, once opened, made us immediately think two things:

1. This is *so* not me.
2. But this would be perfect for _____.

If we can find a warm, accepting home for these errant gifts, wouldn't that make the world a better place?

(Just remember to remove the original "to___/from___" sticker until the rest of the world catches up.)

Xmas-o-phobia

There are weirdnesses in the world that you, Gentle Reader, may not yet have imagined. Exhibit du jour: the Web site www.phobialist.com. Here you will find that there's a "-phobia" for just about anything you can imagine. We could all recognize the names of certain fears (arachnophobia—fear of spiders; claustrophobia—fear of enclosed spaces, etc.), but did you know you could have a fearful condition that you don't even realize you have? Here are a few from the Web site that I did not know were possible:

Triskadekaphobia—fear of the number thirteen
Neophobia—fear of anything new
Peladophobia—fear of bald people
Ecclesiophobia—fear of church
Deipnophobia—fear of dinner conversations
Counterphobia—fear of fears

My fears are different from those of the average person. Some of my personal fears include:

Indecisiphobia—fear related to my indecision regarding a purchase, so that when I finally make up my mind to get the item, I go back and someone else has already taken it

Phonophobia—fear that my SIM card will fail and all my stored numbers will have to be reentered (compounded by the fear that I sync'd recently)

Pedopainophobia—fear that the shoes I really love will, in fact, hurt *worse* than I am projecting they may

If you are suddenly overcome with a wave of fear, it can do things to you physically. My normal adrenal/fear response includes that warm sensation starting at the top of my head simultaneous with a cold, clammy feeling in my extremities. I wonder if clams get a different feeling, or if they just get "clammy-er"?

While I was visiting the phobia Web site, I noticed that there aren't any associated with Christmas, although there are a few that I think should have made that list:

"Ribbonknotaphobia"—the fear that there will be no scissors handy when you are trying desperately to *politely* unwrap the gift your mother-in-law festooned with eight yards of tightly tied curly garland

"Pyrexaphobia"—a fear that you will never get your precious casserole dish returned to you from the neighborhood holiday party

"Visanegaphobia"—the fear you experience while awaiting the approval code on your credit card purchase as you imagine you might be declined due to overlimit issues. This fear causes you to look at the ceiling or stare at your shoes until the approval comes through.

Christmas Memories

$\mathcal{I}$ don't have a great memory. I don't know if I'm so scattered that I don't pay enough attention to adequately catalog them in my mind, or if my memory banks get erased while I'm sleeping, but my family is always recounting things in great detail that I can barely recall. My first inclination was to think that they are setting me up for the opportunity to put me away by making me think I've lost my mind.

I've become more philosophical about my slipping memory. My current mantra is, "If you love a thought, set it free. If it was really yours to begin with, it will come back to you. If it doesn't come back, there's now more room for other thoughts." I think I once thought of making that into a greeting card for the forgetful, but I can't remember if I thought it was a good idea or not.

But there are a couple of Christmases in my childhood that stand out in great detail in my memory bank. One is the year that I got my first bike, with a banana seat and plastic streamers. It was the Christmas that I was six. I still believed in Santa Claus. We lived with my grandparents out in the country, and the roads there were dark and winding. My Uncle Lewis came over and convinced me that if I went for a ride down Mormon Mill Road with him, we might spot Santa and his sleigh, because some of the neighbors had reported seeing Santa in the area. Well, I was beside myself with excitement, and I ran out the door with the absolute knowledge that I was about to see Santa's sleigh with my very own eyes. We drove down the dark roads and I put my face so close to the windshield that my breath fogged it up.

"You keep your eyes peeled for that sleigh," Lewis encouraged me.

The power of suggestion is a strong psychotic force, so I truly believed that I caught a glimpse of Santa at least twice during that ride. About ten minutes later, we were back at the ranch (literally). I burst through the door to tell my mother that I had seen the sleigh, but she started talking first.

"Anita, you'll never believe what just happened! You just missed him. Santa came while you were out, but he left you this bike."

That might have been my first experience with seriously conflicting emotions. I was simultaneously crushed that I had missed him coming to my very own house but speechless at the utter coolness of this bike. Banana seats were the newest, hippest feature that one could have on one's bike, and I was in possession! I immediately concluded that possessing a banana seat trumped witnessing a personal visit from Santa. Besides, I went to sleep secure in the knowledge that I had, indeed, seen him through the fog of Uncle Lewis's windshield.

There is also a photo of me that same Christmas as I sat on a floor with my knees bent and my feet sticking out on each side. I can't begin to re-create that position today, but I recall spending a great deal of my childhood sitting like that on the floor. Flexibility is wasted on the young.

I sat there with some striped slipper socks on my feet, my hair in a headband, and a doll with open-and-shut eyes on my lap. I treasure this picture. It is one of the few photographic remembrances I have of anything remotely girly in my young life. I was surrounded by boy cousins, and most of my playtime was spent with Tonka trucks, miniature front-end loaders, green plastic soldiers, and Hot Wheels. Out in the country, our playtime was spent doing everything outside. We squished a lot of chinaberries, watched a lot of trash burn (we had a chicken-wire cylinder about five feet high and five feet wide where we dumped our trash and burned it down once a week—this is countrified waste management). I have a distinct scar on my right leg that reminds me of when my cousin and I were playing a game that involved jumping over a low piece of barbed wire to see who could do it the most. I lost. Barbies were not on my radar, and my one dolly was a treasure. Until my boy cousins beheaded her.

The Christmas of my ninth year was a standout, too. My mom was dating my future stepfather, the world looked rosier in general, and I received presents that featured electrical cords. This must've been the first year anyone believed that I could utilize a plug-in item without electrocuting myself. But the standards of risk management were different then. We didn't have seat belt laws, our schools were built with asbestos, there was lead in the wall paint of our rooms, *and* we drank tap water. How did we ever survive?

That year I got a Lite-Brite and an Easy-Bake Oven. Life was good. I was gonna make light-up art *and* cook. I was moving up on the Maslow Hierarchy of Girly Needs Chart. The Lite-Brite came with black paper templates to help you make something recognizable (although they only worked once, so if you came up with something you liked, you would leave it up for a week or two; you knew that you could never replicate it). But my favorite Lite-Brite artistic method was to freestyle. I would spell words and make my own designs. Occasionally the Lite-Brite pegs would get stuck in the holes and break as you were pulling them out. That was particularly troublesome when you were down to the end of a design and running out of the color you needed to finish it. In the backwoods in the days before Internet shopping, Lite-Brite replacements were just not gonna happen.

Neither were replacement mixes for the Easy-Bake Oven. You have to hand it to whoever decided that you could put a lightbulb in a painted piece of plastic and pawn it off as a miniature oven. The con certainly worked on me. I saw those commercials during Saturday morning cartoons and I knew that if I had that oven, my eyes would fly open wider than that girl's on the TV as I took the special tool and slid my minicake out the other side. Wouldn't I be the envy of all my boy cousins?

What I didn't realize was that the "mini" part was all too true, and the fifteen minutes that you had to wait for the cake to cool was ten times longer than the cake would last around my cousins. They didn't even let me frost it! And once the three mixes that were included with the oven were history, so was the usefulness of my much-coveted appliance. Such details were not articulated on the commercial. The nearest store that had more mixes was in Austin, fifty miles away from my home. Too far for the banana seat bike.

Bummer.

But the Easy-Bake Oven taught me some important life lessons:

1. Commercials are powerful.
2. Nothing is quite as good as it looks in a commercial.
3. If you stick a small item (such as a ring or a dollar) into an Easy-Bake Oven to hide it from your boy cousins and it falls through the baking rack into the plastic bottom of the oven, you will never get that small item out.

There is one gift I received as an adult that is seared into my memory. This was a gift I gave to myself. I had spent the better part of ten years carting kids from place to place in a Suburban, and Mama was ready to ride a little lower! I wanted an older Jaguar body (on a new car, not on me) in red. I talked to a few reliable sources, and the consensus seemed to be that Jaguar engines were temperamental and expensive to repair, so I figured that a red, decade-old Jag needed to be retrofitted with an American engine.

This was a pretty specific order, wouldn't you say?

But lo and behold, after entering my keywords into an online search engine, said coveted item popped up in south Atlanta. Within a few hours, John and I were down there test-driving the Jag before the bidding opened. I did not win the bidding, but the winning bidder fell through—and the car was mine, mine, mine. How else could this have happened but on eBay?

That's not to say that it didn't turn out to be a long-term-project car, but I do look *very* good sitting in it on the side of the road whenever I am waiting for the tow truck.

The service eBay provides is quite remarkable. Legend has it that some techie built the computer program that runs eBay because his girlfriend was having a hard time finding people in her geographic region to trade with while she quested to expand her Pez dispenser collection. He felt that the time had come to harness the global nature of the Internet for his beloved's desires. Talk about a technical Taj Mahal! Someone finally figured out that in an age with digital photography and Internet access, *no one* should be denied the opportunity to buy anyone's stuff from anywhere on the planet.

And how can you give someone else, someone very dear to you, the gift that *he* will remember always?

I've tried. It's hard.

Year before last, I thought that I had finally found The Gift for John—something that expressed my husband's penchants and would be a source of unending pleasure for him. No, not edible underwear. I found him the Squirrel Defender Bird Feeder.

Oh, how my husband despises squirrels. This hatred may be genetic, since John's dad hates them, too. John and his dad believe that squirrels are deliberately out to undermine a man's dominion of his yard. John's dad wears a sweatshirt upon which squirrels are posed for mug shots; under each mug shot is a description of the squirrel, as if they were "most wanted" criminals.

John also feeds birds in our backyard and cannot *stand* the fact that squirrels will swing from his feeders, spilling the birdseed in greedy attempts to fill their furry little bellies. The sight of squirrels eating from the bird feeder causes John's blood pressure to shoot up at least fifteen points.

So, I found this bird feeder that had a ring around the bottom that was guaranteed to start circling the moment any squirrel dared to venture onto it (like when someone got pitched off the playground merry-go-round in first grade). The box the feeder came in even had a cartoon rendering of people standing around, holding their sides from the hilarious sight of a squirrel being flung off the feeder while the birds dined in peace.

I had happened upon the perfect gift for my husband.

Unfortunately, I didn't read the fine print. Seems that the thing must be regularly charged to keep the slinger a-slingin'. Also, the feeder can't distinguish between skinny squirrels and fat doves. The doves didn't think this feeder was funny at all. The squirrels, meanwhile, were fast learners and, after being slung off only twice, would refuse to go anywhere near the thing. Like most bizarre inventions, the Squirrel Slinger failed to deliver the never-ending joy it promised.

In the end, maybe it's just harder to find a gift for your spouse than for anyone else on your list, a gift that says it all. Maybe it's nearly impossibly difficult to find something that adequately says, "You Are the One, my everything, I love you devotedly."

The only thing I've come up with that makes John's holidays brighter is the "You-can-have-it-every-day-between-Thanksgiving-and-New-Year's" present. Yes. The gift of me not exercising my veto. I cannot tell you how merry this makes him. And how relaxed. It's almost my way of apologizing for all the stress I've caused him all year long. It's not that altruistic, because I'd really rather be dealing with a calm spouse for the holidays. He turns positively Bahamian in his "no problem" satisfied state. Extra relatives staying a few days later than expected? No problem. Dishwasher making funny noises? No problem. Three more parties than I remembered to enter on the weekly planner? No problem. I'm not saying this gift will work for everyone, but a little "charity begins at home" can never be a bad thing, now can it?

The Poinsettia Executioner

$\mathcal{L}$et us turn our attention for a moment to the less attractive aspects of our Christmas rituals. There is, indeed, a Dark Side to the season. There are goings-on no one really wants to discuss openly. This includes the waste. There are the batteries that give of their stored energy and are then tossed aside for new ones. The number of bows that are sitting atop beautifully wrapped packages one day and in the bottom of the Hefty trash bag the next is staggering. The live pines that decorate our homes at least have a second life as they are sent to the chippers to become spring mulch. But today I would like to discuss another form of this senseless waste that hits home for our family: the lowly poinsettia.

I've already established that my man loves Christmas. But in the area of Poinsettia Excess, John is one tortured soul. He feels that a houseful of poinsettias is a necessity of the season, then is tormented by weeks and weeks of sorrow as they all eventually lose their will to live. It is as if they know that they aren't in Mexico anymore. And you can't fool them by playing Spanish language TV, either.

Here is how John's poinsettia disorder got started: He was an associate pastor for most of our married life. In our church we had some Christmas traditions that necessitated a purchase of poinsettias by the truckload. For a few years we had a choral presentation called "The Living Christmas Tree," which consisted of a tall wooden platform several rows high; singers would stand on each row. As this "tree" got taller, the number of people in each row decreased until you got to the top, where there was room for just one. (We always had a skinny, wiry singer at the top, just as you choose someone small for the top of a cheerleader pyramid.) We needed foliage to cover up the wooden edifice, and for The Living Christmas Tree, about two hundred pots of poinsettias sufficed superbly.

We also had a church tradition of offering poinsettias for sale each Christmas in honor of the memory of a loved one. These were nice-size plants wrapped in gold and red foil that covered the plastic pots. Church members would purchase them in bulk (the plants were very reasonably priced, since we received a significant discount for the volume order), and the plants would remain as decorations in the stage area up until the Christmas Eve service, at which time anyone who had made a donation for the poinsettias was welcome to take the flowers home.

Because many of our church members left to visit out-of-state relatives before Christmas Eve, there was always a *bunch* of orphaned poinsettias to deal with. The church offices would be closed for the week, and it fell to my husband (as he was the associate pastor—aka The Minister of Everything Else or The

Minister Who Actually Does All the Work) to find a home for them. He tried valiantly to place as many orphaned poinsettias as possible in good, loving homes. We took as many as we could to shut-ins and nursing homes, but we always had many left over. John couldn't bring himself to let them die alone at the church, so he would bring them home with him. (I am thankful that he doesn't feel the same way about stray cats.)

There were poinsettias everywhere—lining our staircase, on the fireplace hearth, on top of the refrigerator, on the window-sills, on top of the TV, on the nightstands by our bed, and in the bathroom! If there was an open spot, we plugged a pot into it. And when the plants were happy, John was happy.

This bliss lasted about ten days. But as the calendar pages turned to mid-January, our little plants felt that their days of use-fulness were past and began to drop leaves daily. I do not exag-gerate when I tell you that my husband would spend the next eight to ten weeks trying to keep all those plants alive. He would water them, mist them, pick off the dying leaves, talk to them, *anything* to keep them from dying on his watch.

You may be the sort of person who tosses your poinsettias in the trash three days after Christmas and never looks back. Not my John.

And so the Poinsettia Death Watch would commence. It would start with the ones near the fireplace, the first to drop their leaves, because of their proximity to heat. Truth be told, they were the lucky ones. Their demise was quick. Others were not so fortunate.

Some poinsettias seem to be genetically stronger than others. They just don't know when to give up. These determined little fighters would hold on to their colored leaves even when all their green leaves had dropped away. They were no longer lush Christmas décor, but spindly reminders that Valentine's Day could not be more than a week away. John would become sadder and sadder as he became unable to nurse them back to their former glory; he spent way too much time moving the pathetic things around the house to less conspicuous spots. It was too early to transplant them, and besides, we were nowhere near their native Mexican climate. I tried to offer comfort by reminding John that they were only seasonal flora and had had a full and happy life, as flowers go. But he could not bring himself to chuck them.

So it fell to me to be the Poinsettia Executioner. There would always come a day in February when I would take the foil wrappers off the pots and tote them out to the compost pile to return the flowers to the earth from whence they came. It was the least a compassionate soul could do.

In the last few years, John has weaned himself from the Houseful of Poinsettias mind-set and become relatively content with a number somewhere around a dozen. Sure, it's fewer to look at, but for him it's also fewer to grieve over. However, if you happen to see a tall, handsome man with a grocery cart full of poinsettias when the store marks them down on Christmas Eve, it's probably him.

Friends and Cyberfriends

(Or, When You Care Enough to Share Your Primary E-mail Address)

Good friends are like the family you wish you'd had. I've also heard it said that friends are God's way of apologizing for your family. No matter what you think of either, your association with your family and friends will fundamentally change you.

It's important that we have friends who are different from us, otherwise the friendship can be boring, and let's be honest, we have *nothing* to learn from someone who's exactly like us. Researchers have found that having good friends can increase longevity, relieve anxiety, and lower blood pressure. I'm supposing that the opposite is true of a "bad" friend. In fact, you may someday soon be able to get a note from your doctor to give to your "bad" friend stating that you can "no longer be friends for medical reasons."

According to a study published by *The Lancet Neurology*, people with large social circles often score higher on tests *and* they stave off dementia longer. Researchers have no idea why but speculate that maintaining friendships

212

helps build new neural pathways in your brain. So, it's officially medically proven: Friends make you smarter. Any woman knows this is true because the web of knowledge that is woven through a single conversation among more than two friends greatly expands your personal knowledge base (not just facts and figures, but—you know—real human interest stories!). So, if a highly respected journal in medicine says that getting together with friends makes you smarter, then that's just another reason to plan the next girls' night out. When anyone asks you where you're going, tell them it's a little-known branch of Mensa.

Now, the term "friend" may not carry the weight that it has in centuries past with the advent of MySpace and Facebook and the hundred other sites that let you have "friends" via the Internet. It's as if the techies of the world (at their last Preparing for World Domination by Keeping People on Hold for Tech Support Convention) got together and said, "Hey, we have created all these time-saving things that give people hours back in their day (if you don't count all the time we spend downloading updates), so we need to create something to give people something to do with all this found free time and to distract them while we take over the world. What could possibly suck the maximum number of hours out of their lives with absolutely nothing to show for it? Hmmm . . . Eureka! How about creating social networking sites that will benefit almost no one (except Dane Cook—who was the first to build a career on MySpace—and everyone has been trying to do it since, but nobody has) but *will* create a mental itch that people will have to scratch *all day long*?

And these sites will leave their addicts constantly checking in to see if anyone wants to be their friend? Or has commented on their status? Or posted a goofy, pointless video? Brilliant! Let's get our hottest-shot team of cyberheads on it right away!"

Though these Web sites started out for teenagers, the adults of the world have discovered them and, while hoping to regain some shred of their former coolness, caused the teens to flee and start other, cooler sites. While surfing MySpace, I noticed that C. S. Lewis has his own page. You don't even have to be *alive* to do this. If you're dead but interesting, you can still get friends. However, if you're alive and not-so-interesting, you might have problems racking up the online friends. On these pages you can upload information about yourself and upload a few favorite photos, and invite people *you already know* to come and be your friend. Those friends come to your page and leave comments about you, and then other random people who are friends of your friends can post on your page that they would like to be your friend, too, only *now* you have to decide if they are worthy of your friendship based on their friend (who is your mutual friend) and whether or not you want to open yourself up to them and *their* ilk of friends. If you don't like the way their page looks or they just seem like the dodgy sort (meaning that you have perused their page and you can tell that they may be the sort who tend to overpost—like they post every time they inhale and exhale *and* they post without anything witty or cogent to say in response to others' posts), you can *deny* their friendship. Powerful, heady stuff!

Not only can you deny wannabe friends, but you can also rate the friends you have by moving their pictures closer to the top of your list. This tells your friends exactly where they fall in the pecking order.

Do not venture into the world of social networking if you have thin skin because you will get denied, my friend; it's a simple fact. This is the Internet's version of seventh grade, only less subtle. The object is to network with as many friends of friends and collect these people—amass them for reasons that are as yet unclear to me, but it also reminds me of the cardinal party maxim: A friend of a friend may come to a party, but a friend of a friend may not invite *their* friends to the party.

The real power in all of this is just how easily you can delete people. You can deny them in the first place, but that's not all; you can block them once they are your friend and even remove them from your cell phone address book, as if they had never existed. This is the female equivalent to violent video games. We eliminate people with one stroke of "delete." Poof! They're gone. That would be handy in real life, wouldn't it? Maybe we need that on one of those buttons like the THAT WAS EASY Staples button—perhaps one with "delete" and the ability to vaporize office idiots—or maybe just "eject," so you could send them to another department and let someone else deal with them for a change.

Then there are the Twitter-ers. This is social networking on steroids. These are the hard-core addicts who want the world to know every single thought they are thinking and at what time it occurred. They are the purveyors and consumers of FTMI (Far Too Much Information). The terminology for this application is that people "follow" you on Twitter. And you can "follow" them. It's like socially sanctioned Stalker Boot Camp.

CYBERFRIENDS will never replace flesh-and-bone friends. Your Real Friends will always (try to) be there for you. They show up for the tough moments of your life. They aren't afraid to get your mascara on their shoulder, to get into the messy stuff with you. Maybe more importantly they "get" you—and your sense of humor. That's one of the best predictors of a great friendship: whether you find the same things funny. A real friend laughs with you at totally inappropriate times, and isn't inappropriate laughter just one of life's Best Things Ever? You know, that overwhelming feeling you get when you know that you should not be laughing but you just canNOT help yourself? Laughter always seems to hit me at very solemn occasions, like funerals. There really isn't *supposed* to be a lot of laughter at most funerals, but something will invariably happen that leaves me laughing uncontrollably. There are friends at funerals, and the company of friends can make something nominally funny just unbelievably funny. Of course, I put my head down and cover my face with my hand so it seems like I may be *grieving* uncontrollably; usually people who don't know me well can't really tell the difference.

Or during church services. There are so many pastoral verbal faux pas (Or is it "faux pases"? Why wasn't I listening the day we studied pluralizing in French class?) that church should be its own comedy genre. One Sunday evening (Yes, gather round, children, and listen to my tale of when the earth was young and we went to church on Sunday night, too!), when our pastor was teaching on the subject of how God will step into the middle of a situation and turn it around, he listed many stories from the Bible to illustrate how God would step in and intervene in ways that only He could. This pastor explained how God delights in turning around these impossible situations, and we can be clued into these whenever we read in scriptures the words "but God"—this would have been adequate, but he felt the need to elaborate—"and those 'buts' of the Bible are very BIG 'buts.'" I recall the pew shaking as our whole family tried to contain their laughter. All I could think of was how that would make a really great devotional book title, *The Really Big Buts of the Bible.*

But I digress.

The Ultimate Friend Litmus Test is not whether or not you put someone's picture up at the front of your Facebook page, it is whether or not you will come to her home party.

Back when women had more time than money, home parties were a great way to (a) clean your house; (b) show off your house; (c) allow your friends to prove their love by listening to a spiel about stuff they weren't interested in; and (d) further prove their love by opening their checkbook and writing one out for the stuff they were not interested in *and* did not need or want, so that you could meet your goal and get your hostess gift. If for some reason you did not hit your attendance or party orders goal, every woman in your group of friends was highly perturbed at the couple of friends who did not show up and do their part, thus nullifying their sacrifice of attending in the first place.

So everyone repeat this mantra: ONLY YOU CAN PREVENT HOME PARTIES. Yes, my friends, only we can stop such a cycle of madness. It is a cycle, you know: If you go to a friend's party, she has to sign up five people for five more parties in order to get the next level of hostess gift. Then the five people who signed up must each sign up five more people, so it is entirely possible that you would end up having to attend four more shows from your other friends and/or risk having to give one yourself. There is no need for this series of events to perpetuate itself. Here is how we can eradicate it: You are out to dinner or coffee with your friends and one of them gets that gleam in her eye and announces, "Hey, guess what? I'm thinking about having one of those _____ parties." The protocol is that everyone at the table ceases conversation and simultaneously reaches into her purse and pulls out a twenty-dollar bill (or higher, depending on your individual level of loathing for said party type). Lay it on the table and say, "Honey—go out and buy whatever you think you need, 'cause none of us are coming to your party." Done. Finito. The cycle has been broken.

That Bette Midler/Barbara Hershey movie *Beaches*, about women who knew each other for thirty years, shows the power of a long, true friendship. It's good to have those "mafia friends," friends who know so much about you that they cannot be allowed to leave the friendship because of the power of that kind of information. Every girl needs one. These intense friendships are a treasure in life. These are the friends who care about the insane minutiae of your day, won't dump you for random acts of stupidity, listen to your kvetching, aren't scared of your germs, remind you of things you need to be grateful for when you're down, and will go to their graves with your secrets. My friend Kim has been that for me—even though we have been friends in distant cities for longer than we were friends in the same town. Thank God for e-mail and cell phones.

Over a few months, I watched another friend of mine lose *her* best friend of fifty years to a debilitating illness. As her friend was dying, my friend told me how the layers of grief were complicated by sadness for the loss of her friend's life and sadness for the loss of the history they shared together. Losing her friend was like losing a piece of herself.

For more than a decade now, I have been meeting with a group of friends once or twice a year at the beach. These Beach Girls' ages span several decades, and our careers, marriages, children, health, and finances could not be more different. But we are drawn together by deep bonds of affection: We genuinely care about what happens to each other. When we get together, we are allowed to be our most honest, girl-ish selves. We let down and talk about the nitty-gritty of life, bust on it, give different perspectives on it, laugh and cry about it, pray about it, and ultimately admit that none of us really knows what should be done about it. It's so healing to sit in that circle of friends and know that the confidences that pass among us just make our lives more intertwined and inseparable. I wish for every woman some Beach Girls. These are the women who have my back and keep me sane. It's good to have "as-often-as-we-can" friends, too. For me, these are a couple of women I've been meeting with for lunch every month or two for the last seven years. We get together as often as we can and enjoy each other's company. Since we usually end up at the Cheesecake Factory, we refer to ourselves as the "Cheesecake Posse." I know that many of you reading this may not be a part of any community of faith or church, but I have found some of the most enriching friendships of my life to be with those people who were sharing the same spiritual journey and felt a sense of commonality in the mission projects they chose to engage in. It is a wonderful thing to believe that you can leave a lasting legacy in this world, and a community of faith is a great place to find friends who can partner toward that end.

And, by the way, make sure that you have a couple of super-strange people in your mix of friends, because there's nothing better than hanging out with people who are weirder than you are to make you feel more normal.

Anita Rules

There's something about those little personality quizzes that I can't resist. I love the quizzes, the inventories, the matching of column A to column B—whatever the instrument is that promises to tell me why I am the way I am.

I was supercurious about trying to figure out why my three kids are the way they are, so I got *The Birth Order Book* by Kevin Lehman, a book that basically says you are the way you are because of your birth position in the family. This book made sense to me, but what makes more sense is the theory I came up with called "The Room in the Womb Theory." My idea is that you were most impacted by how much room was or was not in the womb when you came along. For instance, my theory asserts, firstborns have a tendency to be overachievers because a previously unoccupied womb would be very, very tight and they would literally have to fight for every single centimeter in there. By contrast, the later-born children (numbers three and four) would have the complete opposite experience. ("Wow—look how nice and roomy it is in here. It looks like someone even put an addition in the back! It's *so* nice and roomy that I think I'll just stretch out and enjoy my life! Yah!") But the middle child, he's a different story. Can't you imagine him floating around in that womb thinking, "Hey . . . it looks like someone might have been in here before me . . . and THAT'S NOT FAIR! I'm gonna get out of here and tell them about everything I think is unfair for the rest of my life!"

But sometimes the birth order stereotypes just don't fit. According to my birth order (only child!), I am a take-charge kinda girl. Why is it then that I just can*not* jump into a swimming pool? This is somewhat embarrassing when the rest of my family dives right in. Not one of them pays any heed to the water temperature. They don't even stick in a toe. They just jump. It's insanity, I tell you.

I'm a *slow pool enterer.* Painfully slow. I don't know why I torture myself this way. My husband, John, always says, "It's easier if you jump in." This is not news to me. I am intellectually aware of this. But as I inch into the water, I must stop short of The Girls. The cold pool water is a shock to them. They want to remain warm; they do not want to be cold and wet. Plus, I have a big nose. I don't like chlorine up my nose, and it doesn't look cool to jump in while holding your nose. Eventually, the negative anticipation becomes overwhelming and I have to take the rest of the plunge (if you can term resentfully dipping the bust to neck area "plunging"). The buildup to this dipping normally lasts about ten minutes. Ten tortured minutes of my life doing what could have been over with in two seconds.

So, of course, all of our behavior isn't determined by birth order. In our household, we call each person's little preferences and predilections his or her "Rules," and, brother, does everyone in our household have his or her own very special set! You can identify your Rules by filling in "Never/Always" statements ("I never _____." "I always _____."). Anyone reading this who is in denial about the fact that you *have* Rules has as personal Rule Number 1: "I never have any rules."

I will start with myself (just to be fair). I have a rule about the tops of things. I like them. Just the tops. Not the bottoms. I like just the tops of muffins. Not the part that would be contained in the muffin cup, but the top part that's just a little bigger than the cup. I also like the top bite of a banana. I like to lie with one leg on top of the covers, and I dig the foam on top of a cappuccino. Other Anita Rules? I always take more clothes than I need to take on a trip (I like options, because I dress emotionally and I never know how I might feel on any given day), and I never file papers immediately. I feel they need to sit out in the open air for a while before they are crushed in the cruel file folders forever.

John's Rules include: No items of mine should ever be on his side of the bed, and no one can enter his closet or touch his things without him hyperventilating. He must have corn bread with greens, and he cannot discard a *Sports Illustrated* until it has been in the bathroom three weeks.

My mom's Rules are that no one may come to the kitchen in the morning without bringing their dirty clothes with them (because, as we all know, dirty clothes mate if left unsupervised and produce *more* dirty clothes). Also, all dishes must be heated before the hot food or beverages can be served in them. I am not sure if she was very cold for long periods of time as a child or what, but the coffee cups and carafe have to be heated up (with hot water from the microwave) before the coffee can be brewed, and the plates for dinner have to be heated up so that the food won't cool off too soon. Never mind that we are all burning our fingers on the hot edges. She would have them sizzling like the fajita plates at the Mexican restaurant if she had her way. She also has no respect for John's closet Rule and goes in there when we are out of town to hang up his ironed shirts.

Our eldest, Calvin, has one about replacing his expended calories immediately after a workout. We can be twenty minutes away from serving a big dinner and Calvin will be over in the corner of the kitchen with the blender, whipping up his power shake because he just came back from lifting weights. I'll look at him and say, "But we're eating in twenty minutes," and he'll say, "Mom, you know I have to do this." It's a Rule. Calvin also must be with people all the time. If he is awake, there must be a friend or co-worker within range. This is only temporarily interrupted by school or work activities, but, of course, he makes friends at school or work so that he can continue to enforce this Rule. Also, if you happen to stand between him and the TV when the ESPN channel is on, he gets highly agitated.

Austin's first Rule is that he never wants to stop whatever he is doing. I have no idea why this is, but whatever he is doing at the moment is the most important thing he has ever done, and he perceives any interruption in the doing of that thing as a direct threat. It doesn't matter if the thing you are asking that he start doing is his favorite thing in the world, he doesn't want to stop doing the current thing to do the alternate thing. It's as if he has no personal "clutch" to shift from one activity to the next, and you can almost hear the mental gears "grinding" while he struggles through the transition. At that point, whatever the new activity is *becomes* the one he is now committed to and doesn't want to stop. Austin also has a Rule about Most Favored Outfit Status. If a particular outfit is one that he is enamored of, he is capable of wearing it over and over again. And again. Come to think of it, that's just an extension of his Rule Number 1.

Now we come to Baby Girl Elyse, the Ruler of All Rulers. She has a Rule for just about every letter of the alphabet. Her sheets and covers can't ever touch the floor (there are bugs down there), she will only drink out of glasses with pleasing shapes, she never sets her purse on the floorboards of cars, she always gets upset if someone touches her hair, and she never likes to pack her shoes in the same suitcase as her clothes. One Rule she and I share is the reading of the virgin magazines. (This is when a magazine is freshest and the best information is available only for the first person who reads it. If a magazine has already been read by someone else, it loses its thrill.)

I suppose a lot of people would think all that stuff is what makes us weird. I've personally never had that big of a problem with weirdness, or eccentricities. Those are the things that not only let you know you're not just another one off the assembly line, but also make you identifiable, irascible, and wholly you. I'm sure none of us truly "gets" why others are the way they are. But I'm not sure that it matters if we "get it"—it only matters if we love others in spite of the things we don't understand about them. That's one level. Another we could aspire to is to love them *because* of all that stuff we don't understand. Once we embrace our own inner weirdnesses, we are truly capable of loving the eccentricities in others, some of them under our own roof.

Embrace your inner weirdness.

It will give 'em stuff to talk about at your funeral.

AFTERWORD

*H*ardly anyone reads the books they buy.

At least, not all the way to the end.

Some get several pages in and decide they just don't have the stamina to go the distance.

The sad fact is that a lot of books are like cruise passengers who never disembark from the boat: They go a lot of places but never really enjoy any of them. First a book's owner falls in love with the title or cover, so she buys the book and takes it to her car. But since the book's in the backseat in a bag, it doesn't make it into the house for a good while. Instead, it languishes in the hot sun and lies there, abandoned, through dark, cold nights, buried beneath a couple of McDonald's bags and a pile of stuff to be dropped off at Goodwill. When the book is finally rediscovered by its owner, she is past the cooling-off period of love for the title or the cover, and she questions why she was so attracted to the book in the first place. The book then makes the rounds from the entryway to the bedside to the book tote to the bookshelf to the beach to a friend to the friend's car, where the cycle starts all over again.

If a book makes it into a house and stays there, it often just lies around so the owners can appear to be literary types.

But you are better than those other people. You have read this book.

You didn't read your favorite line aloud to your co-worker, then cave to the pressure to let her "borrow" it for a while. (Those book borrowers never give them back!)

No. You read the whole book. You did it. You are about to read the last line.

You're no quitter. You are legend.

Feel your superior-ness. Feel it deep.